DEPARTMENT CHAIR LEADERSHIP SKILLS

By Walter H. Gmelch and Val D. Miskin

Atwood Publishing
Madison, WI

Department Chair Leadership Skills
By Walter H. Gmelch and Val D. Miskin
ISBN: 978-1-891859-79-3

© 2011, Atwood Publishing, Madison, Wisconsin
www.atwoodpublishing.com

Cover design by Tamara Dever, TLC Graphics, www.tlcgraphics.com

Library of Congress Cataloging-in-Publication Data

Gmelch, Walter H.
 Department chair leadership skills / by Walter H. Gmelch and Val D. Miskin.
    p. cm.
 Includes bibliographical references and index.
 Rev. ed. of: Leadership skills for department chairs : Bolton, MA. : Anker Pub.
Co.,1993.
 ISBN 978-1-891859-79-3 (pb)
 1. College department heads—Handbooks, manuals, etc. 2. Educational
leadership—Handbooks, manuals, etc. I. Miskin, Val D., 1944- II. Gmelch, Walter
H., Leadership skills for department chairs. III. Title.
 LB2341.G56 2011
 378.1'11—dc22
                         2010034755

TABLE OF CONTENTS

Chapter 1

THE CALL FOR LEADERSHIP

Even if you're on the right track,
you'll get run over if you just sit there.
—Will Rogers

The time of "amateur administration"—where professors play musical chairs, stepping occasionally into the role of department chair—is over. Too much is at stake in this time of change and challenge to let leadership be left to chance or taking turns. The department chair position is the most critical role in the university, and the most unique management position in America. Consider the facts: 80 percent of university decisions are made at the department level (Carroll and Wolverton 2004); of the 50,000 chairs in America, one in five turn over every year; and while it takes 10,000 hours of practice to reach competence (projected as eight years for chairs and already established as seven years for faculty to get tenure) (Thomas and Schuh 2004), only 3 percent of chairs receive training in leadership (Gmelch et al. 2002).

In higher education, the development of academic leaders is at a critical juncture. While the corporate world complains that it has simply progressed from the Bronze Age of leadership development to the Iron Age (Conger and Benjamin 1999), we fear that in higher education we may still be in the Dark Ages (Gmelch 2000b). It is our hope that this book will illuminate the way to the Building Age of our leadership capacity in departments, colleges, and universities.

The search for solutions to academia's leadership dilemma leads us to realize that the academic leader is the least studied and most misunderstood management position in America. The preparation of academic leaders takes time, training, commitment, and expertise. One of the most glaring shortcomings in the leadership area is the scarcity of sound research on the training and development of leaders (Conger and Benjamin 1999; Gmelch 2000b). Academic leaders tend to begin their careers in research and teaching; as researchers and teachers, they scarcely anticipate their current leadership positions, and become chairs with only minimal management training (Hecht 2004). We reward our new PhDs for becoming internationally renowned experts in narrow fields, then complain that few are willing or prepared to be generalists who serve in a leadership capacity.

This chapter addresses the why, what, and how of the leadership call. In essence, it attempts to answer three basic questions: 1) Why become a department chair? 2) What do department chairs do? 3) How can you become an effective chair?

WHY BE A DEPARTMENT CHAIR?

Given the obstacles, complications, and ambiguities of the chair position, why do faculty members choose to serve in this capacity? What are the real motives faculty members have for accepting the position, and do their motivations affect their willingness to be leaders?

As you examine your own motives, it may help to see responses from others concerning their decisions to become department chairs. Over the past two decades, numerous studies conducted by the Center for Academic Leadership (formerly the Center for the Study of the Department Chair), using both interviews and surveys, offer insight into this decision and how it affects the leadership role. When chairs across the United States were asked what motivated them to become department chairs, they basically responded in two ways.

Extrinsic motivation

Some chairs chose to serve for *extrinsic* reasons: either their deans or colleagues convinced them to take the job, or they felt forced to take it because no one else was willing or able. Typically, the testimonials of extrinsically motivated respondents indicated that they were approached by the dean. One chair said: "Temporary insanity (only kidding); the dean approached me—said he thought I had a lot of skills that were needed and that I could do a good job" (Seedorf 1990). Other chairs were persuaded by their peers because "no one else had a suitable combination of seniority, respect, and personality." Some chairs took the position because they felt that they could do a better job than other faculty: "No one who would be a good chair was interested," or "None of those who were interested were, in my opinion, capable of being a good chair—I was scared to death of the alternative!" (Seedorf 1990).

Intrinsic motivation

By contrast, many chairs sought the position for *intrinsic* reasons: they saw it as an opportunity to help either their departments or themselves. Those who expressed the altruistic need to help the department stated that they "desired to help other faculty members," "wanted to build a strong academic department," or "needed to help develop a new program in the department." Others who were more motivated by personal reasons sought the chair position because they "needed a challenge," "required the financial gain (if there really is any!)," "desired to try something new … in addition to teaching and research," "wanted administrative experience in order to take the next step in the career ladder," or simply "wanted to be in more control of [their] environment."

Does the initial motivation affect the chair's ability or willingness to serve? In the national survey (Gmelch et al. 1990), hundreds of chairs answered the following two questions: "What was your motivation to serve?" and "Are you willing to serve more than one term?" The results, reported in Table 1.1, indicate that chairs most frequently served for personal development reasons (321 chairs, or 60 percent). However, 251 (46.8 percent) of the chairs said they also were drafted by their dean or colleagues. These were the two most frequent reasons for serving as department chair—the former represents an intrinsic motivation and the latter an extrinsic motivation.

In response to the second question, 46 percent of the chairs said they would serve another term, 30 percent said they would not, and 24 percent were undecided (Figure 1.1). What is interesting is that those who agreed to serve primarily for extrinsic reasons were the least likely to serve another term (only 25 percent, see Figure 1.2). In contrast, three quarters of the intrinsically motivated chairs were willing to serve again (Figure 1.3). By a three-to-one margin, those most willing to continue in the chair position had taken the position for personal-intrinsic reasons.

Table 1.1 Why Faculty Become Department Chairs

REASON FOR SERVING	NUMBER OF CHAIRS
1. For personal development (interesting, challenge, new opportunities)	321
2. Drafted by the dean or my colleagues	251
3. Out of necessity (lack of alternative candidates)	196
4. To be more in control of my environment	161
5. Out of sense of duty, it was my turn	133
6. For financial gain	117
7. An opportunity to relocate at new institution	101

Source: Center for the Study of the Department Chair, Washington State University (Gmelch et al. 1990)

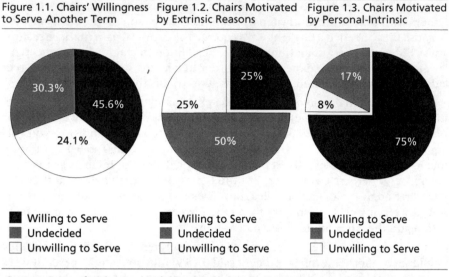

Figure 1.1. Chairs' Willingness to Serve Another Term

Figure 1.2. Chairs Motivated by Extrinsic Reasons

Figure 1.3. Chairs Motivated by Personal-Intrinsic

- ■ Willing to Serve
- ▨ Undecided
- □ Unwilling to Serve

- ■ Willing to Serve
- ▨ Undecided
- □ Unwilling to Serve

- ■ Willing to Serve
- ▨ Undecided
- □ Unwilling to Serve

Source: Center for the Study of the Department Chair, Washington State University (Gmelch et al. 1990)

What about the chairs' satisfaction with their institutions and departents? When almost a thousand chairs were asked to rate their departments, the vast majority expressed a high degree of satisfaction: 98 percent rated the quality of their faculty as "average to excellent;" 90 percent rated the personal relations among faculty in their departments as "average to excellent;" and 97 percent rated the relations with students as "average to excellent." Few, less than 3 percent, rated these categories as "poor." Regarding their institutions, three quarters of the department chairs rated the intellectual climate and quality of administration as "average to excellent" (86 percent and 71 percent, respectively). The only area with which department chairs expressed less than high satisfaction was salary (42 percent "below average"). Basically, department chairs are highly satisfied with their institutions and departments, but feel plagued by excessive stress and unresolved conflicts (see chapters 6 and 7).

Regardless of your initial reasons for agreeing to serve as chair, your current motivation and commitment to continuing in administration will influence your ability to develop leadership capacity. Reflect for a moment and indicate in Exercise 1.1 the primary reasons you became a department chair.

Given the current leadership crisis in higher education, it is critical for department chairs to answer the leadership call. There needs to be continuity in the chair position, not just taking one's turn. The position of department chair is too critical to the effectiveness of the institution, the faculty, the community, and to you personally to serve solely from a sense of duty. Your sense of duty

---

Exercise 1.1. Why Be a Department Chair?

Indicate below the reasons why you became department chair. You may check more than one.

_____ 1. For personal development (challenge, new opportunities)

_____ 2. For more control of my environment

_____ 3. For financial gain

_____ 4. Drafted by the dean or my colleagues

_____ 5. Out of a sense of duty: it was my turn

_____ 6. Out of necessity: lack of alternative candidate

Now compare your responses with those of other chairs in Table 1.1.

---

must be combined with a real commitment to the position, with all its challenges and responsibilities.

WHAT DO CHAIRS DO?

No doubt you keep busy as department chair. Endless meetings, stacks of paperwork, constant interruptions, and fragmented encounters on a multitude of topics set a frantic pace. But to what end? All the memos, meetings, phone calls, drop-in visitors, and confrontations represent *means*, but do these activities produce the desired *ends*?

You must understand that effective chairs influence the futures of their departments. It is the focus on results that successfully moves departments through these changing times. Virtually every managerial book ever written lists and exults the tasks, duties, roles, and responsibilities of administrators—from the traditional Peter Drucker approach of planning, organizing, staffing, delegating, and controlling, to Warren Bennis's four elements of transformational leadership: attention through vision, meaning through communication, trust through positioning, and the deployment of self (Bennis and Nanus 1985).

Lists specific to department chair duties range from the exhaustive listing of 97 activities identified by a University of Nebraska research team (Creswell et al. 1990), to the astonishing 54 varieties of tasks and duties cited in Allan Tucker's classic book *Chairing the Academic Department* (1992), to the 40 functions forwarded in a study of Australian department chairs (Moses and Roe 1990). The genesis of these lists can be traced back to Siever's 12 functions, expanded to 18 by McCarthy, reduced to 15 by Hoyt, and expanded again to 27 by Smart and Elton (Moses and Roe 1990).

Typical faculty manuals at colleges and universities provide a list of the chairs' duties and responsibilities, such as organizing and supervising curriculum, distributing teaching/research loads, supervising department funds, recommending promotions and salaries, and so on. Check your college manual for your own local listings! While these numerous lists appear refined and comprehensive, they continue to represent fragmented activities without focus on what's most important—the results.

The four roles of department chairs

Which roles are critical for department chairs who want results? In answer to this question, four main roles emerge from the popular literature and converge with current research: the Faculty Developer, the Manager, the Leader, and the Scholar (see Gmelch and Miskin 2004 for further discussion of department chair roles).

The role of *Faculty Developer* is viewed by department chairs as their most important responsibility. It involves recruiting, selecting, and evaluating faculty, as well as providing the sort of informal leadership that enhances the faculty's morale and professional development.

Acting as *Manager*, the second role, is a requirement of the position, but often least liked by chairs. Chairs spend over half the week in departmental activities. Specifically, they perform the upkeep-functions of preparing budgets, maintaining department records, assigning duties to faculty, supervising non-academic staff, and maintaining finances, facilities, and equipment.

Leader best describes the third role of department chairs. As leaders of their departments, they provide long-term direction and vision, solicit ideas for department improvement, plan and evaluate curriculum development, and plan and conduct departmental meetings. They also provide external leadership for their departments by working with their constituents to coordinate department activities, representing their departments at professional meetings and, on behalf of their departments, participating in college and university committees to keep faculty informed of external concerns. Chairs seem to like this role, because it offers opportunities to help others develop professional skills, to stay challenged, and to influence the profession and department. Those chairs who enjoy such leadership activities spend more time performing them —not a surprising revelation! It is our hope that not only do department chairs enjoy this role, but that they take it most seriously when assuming their administrative position. Since it is the most critical role in achieving success, the entire second section of this book is devoted to the call to leadership.

In contrast to the managerial nature of the three previous roles, chairs also try to remain a *Scholar*. This includes teaching and staying current in their academic disciplines and, for those at research universities, maintaining an active research program and obtaining grants to support it. Chairs enjoy and feel most comfortable in this role, but express frustration with their inability to spend much time on their academic interests. Many would emphasize scholarship if they could, but find it virtually impossible. In fact, 86 percent of department chairs significantly reduce their scholarly activities while serving as chair; for some, scholarship more or less ceases (Gmelch and Miskin 2004).

Where do your primary interests lie? Exercise 1.2 enables you to assess the degree to which each of these four roles is important to you. In order to obtain a sense of identity, reflect for a moment on how you ranked the four roles, then identify the most important tasks by which you obtain results within each role. Is your perception of your job in line with the reality of the results you get? If not, you may have to realign some of your time and energy to maximize your results. These adjustments should be made consciously as you assume the administrative role of department chair. The transition from the professorial role to that of department chair is vital to your success.

HOW CAN YOU BE AN EFFECTIVE CHAIR?

While it would be convenient to move immediately into your leadership role, the transformation from professor to chair takes time and dedication. Not all chairs make the complete transition. They try to maintain their faculty responsibilities during their time in office and engage in both types of work simultaneously. This tends not to work well; as one researcher put it, "the work of administration and the work of the professor do not make good bedfellows.... The nature of administrative work is varied, brief, and fragmented, and therefore, the administrator cannot devote long periods of uninterrupted time to single issues. The nature of professorial work demands long periods of time to concentrate on issues, to write and see a work through to publication, and to prepare to teach and evaluate classes" (Seedorf 1990, 122-123). You must let go of your previous professorial role, at least in part, in order to make this transition successfully. This underscores the importance of wanting to serve for the right reasons. Intrinsic motivation may indeed be a prerequisite to accepting the leadership challenge.

Transitions to leadership

The drastic differences between the roles of scholar and administrator help explain the difficulty in making the transition to department chair. As this transformation—aptly termed the "metamorphosis of the department chair"—takes place, several of your "faculty" functions and work habits change into "chair" work-styles (Gmelch and Miskin 2004; Gmelch and Seedorf 1989). These new chair work-styles are much different from what you were used to as a faculty member and will take some adjustment. The following list outlines nine transitions you face when moving from a faculty position to department chair.

1. *From solitary to social.* College professors typically work alone on research, teaching preparation, and projects. Now, as chair, your

Exercise 1.2. Department Chair Role Orientation Instrument

CHAIR ROLE

A. Listed below are 24 typical duties of department chairs. Please answer the following questions for each of the duties listed.

	Of what importance is each duty?				
	Low			High	

Leader

Coordinate department activities with constituents	1	2	3	4	5
Plan and evaluate curriculum development	1	2	3	4	5
Solicit ideas to improve the department	1	2	3	4	5
Represent the department at professional meetings	1	2	3	4	5
Inform faculty of department, college, and university concerns	1	2	3	4	5
Develop and initiate long-range department goals	1	2	3	4	5

Scholar

Obtain resources for personal research	1	2	3	4	5
Maintain research program and associated professional activities	1	2	3	4	5
Remain current within academic discipline	1	2	3	4	5
Obtain and manage external funds (grants, contracts)	1	2	3	4	5
Select and supervise graduate students	1	2	3	4	5
Teach and advise students	1	2	3	4	5

Faculty Developer

Encourage professional development efforts of faculty	1	2	3	4	5
Provide informal faculty leadership	1	2	3	4	5
Encourage faculty research and publication	1	2	3	4	5
Recruit and select faculty	1	2	3	4	5
Maintain conducive work climate, including reducing conflicts	1	2	3	4	5
Evaluate faculty performance	1	2	3	4	5

Manager

Prepare and propose budgets	1	2	3	4	5
Manage department resources (finances, facilities, equipment)	1	2	3	4	5
Ensure the maintenance of accurate department records	1	2	3	4	5
Manage nonacademic staff	1	2	3	4	5
Assign teaching, research, and other related duties to faculty	1	2	3	4	5
Write department reports and memos	1	2	3	4	5

ROLE-ORIENTATION SCORING

The Department Chair Role Orientation Instrument is keyed to four different roles department chairs perform.

B. Add your total score for each role. Plot your scores on the appropriate axes on the next page; then connect the points with straight lines to get a visual representation of the web you are weaving as a department chair. What are your dominant and backup chair roles?

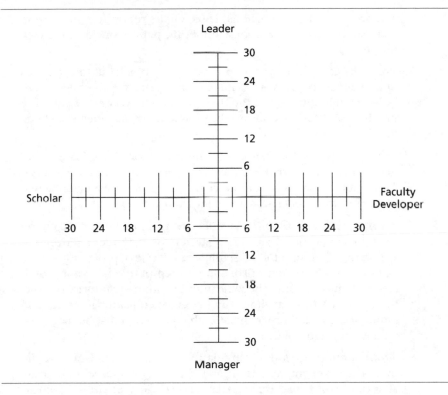

responsibilities force you to work with and through others. For example, department goals cannot be achieved alone, they must be achieved in concert with your faculty.

2. *From focused to fragmented.* While professors must have long, uninterrupted periods to work on scholarly pursuits, your work as department chair, like other management positions, is characterized by brevity, variety, and fragmentation.

3. *From autonomy to accountability.* Professors generally enjoy control over their time and the feeling of autonomy of activity and movement in their working environment. As you move from your role of professor to administrator you tend to lose this sense of autonomy, and become accountable to upper administration and the faculty for your time and accessibility in the office, as well as for your actions and activities.

4. *From manuscripts to memoranda.* The scholar and researcher labors over a manuscript for a long period of time. Before finding printer's ink, the work goes through many revisions and critiques. As department chair you must quickly learn the art of persuasion

and precision through memos. Thus, chairs report less stress from manuscripts and more from completing paperwork on time (see chapter 7).

5. *From private to public.* The professor may block out long periods of time for scholarly work, while as chair you have an obligation to be accessible throughout the day. In essence, you move from the privilege of a "closed door" to the obligation of an "open door" policy.

6. *From professing to persuading.* The professor disseminates information in a manner that will meet the learning objectives of others. As you turn from professor into chair, you profess less and practice more the art of persuasion and compromise.

7. *From stability to mobility.* While always growing and exploring new concepts and ideas, faculty generally experience movement within the stability of their discipline and circle of professional associations. As a chair, you will of course attempt to retain your professional identity, but must become mobile within the university structure. In order to be at the cutting edge of educational reform and implement needed programmatic changes, you must be more mobile, visible, and political.

8. *From client to custodian.* In relation to university resources, the professor is a client, requesting and expecting resources to be available to conduct research, classes, and service activities. As chair, you represent the custodian and dispenser of resources. You are responsible for the maintenance of the physical setting, as well as providing material and money.

9. *From austerity to prosperity.* While the pay differential between professor and chair may not actually be significant, the perception that chairs have more control over departmental resources creates the illusion that chairs are more prosperous.

Rather than listing these transitions in a table, Figure 1.4 visually places the professor at the inner core of a set of concentric circles. The professor is characterized in this inner circle as focused, autonomous, private, stable, solitary, austere, and a client of the department. The metamorphosis transforms these professorial inner traits into an other-oriented (outer circle), creating an administrative profile of social, fragmented, accountable, public, mobile, prosperous, and custodial. These outwardly expanding circles represent the types of transitions needed to successfully move from a faculty member to administrative responsibility and challenge. You must recognize the fundamental differences between the roles of academic professor and department chair.

Figure 1.4. The Transformation from Professor to Chair

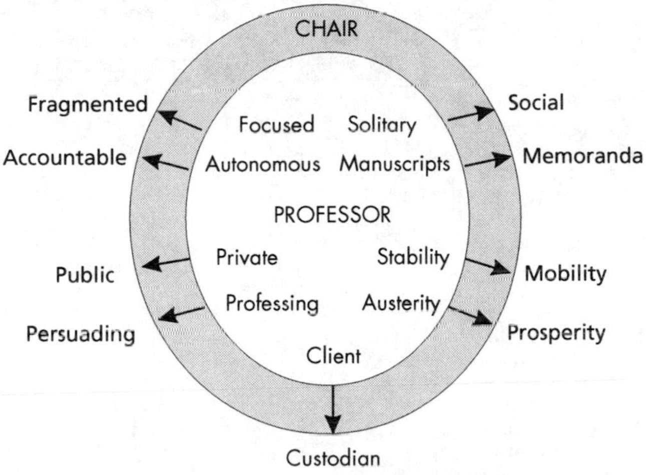

ARE YOU READY FOR DEPARTMENT LEADERSHIP?

Leadership self-assessment

Regardless of gender, minority status, or ethnic heritage, the process of improving your leadership capacity will:

- place value on diversity in experience and talent;
- encourage staff to participate and satisfy their interests;
- build a collective team climate.

An honest self-appraisal of your management style can be most beneficial in assessing how ready you are for this leadership challenge. Rate yourself on the items in Exercise 1.3. Express your current attitudes toward openness, recognition, diverse perspectives, and faculty development, and you will discover your readiness to enjoy your role as department chair. These ratings give an overall indication of your willingness to accept leadership responsibilities while maintaining the respect of your faculty members.

Calculate your score by adding the total items checked in each of the four columns. Then multiply the first (leftmost) column's total by one, the second column's total by two, the third column's total by three, and the fourth column's total by four. Adding these new totals together will give you your department-leadership score.

If you score below twenty-five, you may want to set some specific improvement goals for yourself. A score of thirty-five or above indicates a strong

Exercise 1.3. Department-Leadership Self-Assessment

REQUIRED LEADERSHIP BEHAVIORS	(1) Not Really True	(2) Could Use Improvement	(3) Partially True	(4) Very True
A. Able to show visible enthusiasm for almost all duties of the department chair				
B. Willing to put in significant extra time if necessary to prepare for an upcoming faculty meeting				
C. Able to put in considerably more work than any other faculty members without feeling resentment				
D. Able to direct attention and efforts toward department goals, even at the expense of own personal interests				
E. Recognize the benefit of diverse perspectives and participation, even if it means increased conflict				
F. Able to give direction when needed without taking over (dominating) the functions of the staff				
G. Willing to give attention and praise to all faculty members whenever they are deserving				
H. Concerned with each faculty member's current abilities, goals, and attitudes toward department success				
I. Willing to rely on the achievements of faculty for own recognition from higher management				
J. Able to guide all faculty members effectively in new areas				
Subtotal=	(x1)	(x2)	(x3)	(x4)
TOTAL DEPARTMENT LEADERSHIP SCORE				

foundation for guiding your faculty's and department's vitality. You are now on your way to answering the call to leadership.

THE CALL FOR ACADEMIC LEADERS

Historically, academic leaders appear to be more and more responsible for extramural funding, personnel decision making, and alumni relations. The vision of an academic leader (e.g., lead faculty member or department chair) as a quiet, scholarly type has largely been overtaken by the image of an executive who is politically astute and economically savvy. Being both a faculty member and an administrator is a terribly difficult balancing act. Today's leader in the academy resembles a species with an imperiled existence.

Obstacles to the call for academic leadership

Why do some professors choose to lead and others not? What conditions do we create in higher education that act as barriers to attracting academics to leadership positions (Gmelch and Miskin 2004)?

Snuff out the spark before the leadership flame is ignited. Our institutions of higher education have themselves to blame. If a spark of enthusiasm for leadership is ignited in any of our young faculty, our institutional system may well snuff it out (Gardner 1987). We consider the need for experts and professionals greater than the need for leaders. Many academics might prefer an institution in which there were no leaders whatsoever, only experts; far from wishing to be leaders, these academics may not even wish to associate with one. We fail to cultivate leadership talent in our junior faculty. We pay little attention to structuring academic leadership duties/opportunities, offering role models, and providing ongoing reinforcement and guidance in leadership skills and competencies.

Exalt the prestige and prowess of the professional expert. Some academics may possess the requisite skills and leadership ability, but choose not to respond to the call (Boyatzis 1990). The prestige of one's professional discipline drains off potential leaders into "marvelously profitable non-leadership roles" (Gmelch and Miskin 2004). From graduate school onward, institutions of higher education drive academics down the road to specialization, but academic leaders must be generalists. "Tomorrow's leaders will very likely have begun life as trained specialists, but to mature as leaders they must sooner or later climb out of the trenches of specialization and rise above the boundaries that separate the various segments of society" (Gardner 1987, 7). Administrators must be generalists to cope with a diversity of problems and a multitude of constituencies; they must approach the academy with a broader, more systematic vision.

Ignore the rigors of public and personal life. Many faculty join the academy in search of a professional life characterized by autonomy and independence. They observe the stormy years of chairs, the scathing criticisms of other academic leaders (deans and presidents), and wonder, "Why would I want to subject myself to such scrutiny and public criticism?" We cannot ensure much personal privacy for chairs, as they serve the public every moment of the day, with all of their appointments, messages, and memos open to scrutiny, critique, comment, and review. Even at home, academics find that leadership is not a "family friendly" profession. Thus, most academics are not willing to give up their professional and personal lives for the life of servanthood/leadership.

Precarious state of executive selection. Experts contend that the state of selection of the top three levels of the organization is precarious at best (Sessa and Taylor 2000). In higher education, that typically includes presidents, provosts, and deans, although one might even question the state of selecting department chairs. Why? First, universities and colleges have very little expertise in the selection of leaders, and at times leave that process to happenstance or executive search firms. Second, executives themselves do not feel particularly competent in the skills needed in selection, and gravitate instead to pressing, day-to-day needs. Finally, most institutions of higher education have inadequate hiring, training, promotional, and succession-planning systems.

THE DEVELOPMENT OF ACADEMIC LEADERS

As noted earlier, one of the most glaring shortcomings in the leadership area is the scarcity of sound research on the training and development of leaders (Conger and Benjamin 1999). The head of a large corporation once said: "We recruit people fresh out of college, and for thirty years we reward them for keeping their noses to the grindstone, doing their narrow jobs unquestionably. Then when a top post opens up, we look around in frustration and say 'Where are the statesmen?' No one consciously intended to eliminate the statesman; but the organizational culture produced that result" (Gardner 1987, 19). We do the same in higher education, socializing and rewarding our new PhD's to become internationally renowned experts in narrow fields, then complaining that no one is willing or prepared to be a generalist and serve in a leadership capacity.

Spheres of chair-development

We do not name these obstacles, motivations, transformations, and conflicting roles in an attempt to dampen the call to leadership, but as a first step in addressing the challenges we must overcome in order to develop our next generation of department chairs. Given these challenges, how do we send a call out to awaken the latent leaders in the academy? How do we make some academics aware of their leadership potential? How do we make leadership feasible, tolerable, and inviting for academics? Rather than search for answers in specific training programs, we outline three spheres of influence that are essential to the development of effective academic leaders: 1) conceptual understanding of the unique roles and responsibilities encompassed by academic leadership; 2) the skills necessary to achieve results through working with faculty, staff, students, and other administrators; and 3) the practice of reflection in order to learn from past experiences and perfect the art of leadership (Gmelch and Miskin 2004). These three spheres and their intersections (see Figure 1.4) serve as our analytical framework for determining what is needed to develop department chairs.

Conceptual understanding. Conceptual understanding is the ability to see leadership in terms of mental models (Senge 1990), frameworks (Bolman and Deal 2003), and roles (Gmelch and Miskin 2004). These categories will allow chairs to grasp, cognitively, the many dimensions of leadership (Conger and Benjamin 1999). The most important challenges addressed by these categories are:

1. As managers move into leadership positions, the concept of the job shifts. Academics moving into the role of department chair start to perceive themselves differently. For example, using Lee Bolman and Terry Deal's terms (2003), department chairs initially think in terms of their human and structural frames of leadership; as they gain comfort and confidence, two new frames demand greater attention: the political and the symbolic.

2. Institutions of higher education have unique challenges not typical of managers and leaders in other organizations. The position of department chair has been characterized as without parallel in the business world. Department chairs cultivate external/political relationships, manage college resources, promote internal productivity, attend to personnel matters, and engage in personal scholarship. Some of these roles are unique to the academy (e.g., personal scholarship) while others represent new responsibilities that chairs accept when they move up the hierarchy.

Whether it is in terms of frames, roles, responsibilities, models, or tasks, chairs need to understand the dimensions of their position. Universities typically teach *others* to understand leadership conceptually. The time has come for us to teach academics how they can become leaders in their own domain. Chairs, especially, need to define academic leadership for themselves: what does it mean to build a community, empower others, and set direction? Of course, while a conceptual understanding of department chair roles is a condition of leadership, it is not sufficient without the application of appropriate behaviors and skills.

Skill development. In order to perform their roles and meet their responsibilities, chairs need to hone their skills. To this end, a recent proliferation of books on department chairs suggests tips, techniques, and promising practices (see Buller 2006; Chu 2006; Lee 2006; Wheeler et al. 2008). Reading often reminds leaders more than it instructs them, but department chairs can "formally"

Figure 1.4. Department Chair Leadership Development

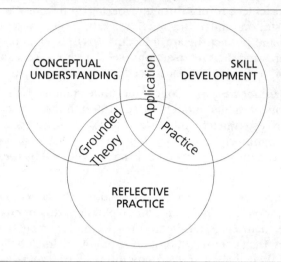

learn to develop their leadership skills through clinical approaches: seminars, workshops, and lecturettes. These approaches impart principles that chairs can put into practice through simulations, case studies, role-playing, and action planning. Some skills, such as communication, performance coaching, conflict resolution, negotiation, and resource deployment are more readily teachable than complex competencies, like strategic vision, that have a long gestation period and involve multiple aptitudes (Conger 1992; Westley 1992; Wheeler et al. 2008).

Many training programs for academic leaders are off-site, last three to four days, and are designed for institutions' mid-managers. While these can instill key ingredients for skill development, research has shown that it is more effective for work teams to attend the same programs as their supervisors, such that each supports and reinforces the other's skill-building efforts (Conger 1992).

Formal training is only one part of acquiring key skills. Individuals often require on-the-job experience to translate their understanding of a skill from intellectual to personal, after which they can apply the skill practically. Recall the aphorism of the Chinese philosopher: *To know and not to use, is not yet to know*. Experience is critical to skill building and takes many forms, such as experimenting, receiving feedback, coaching, refining, and perfecting (Ericsson and Smith 1991).

Reflective practice. It's not enough to understand the roles of a department chair and the skills required to be successful. Leadership development, often the most difficult part of professional growth, is an inner journey. Self-knowledge, personal awareness, and corrective feedback must be part of chairs' leadership journey. Moral, ethical, and spiritual dimensions are necessary for the journey's completion. Leadership development is very much about finding one's voice (Kouzes and Posner 1987). Because credibility and authenticity lie at the heart of leadership, finding one's own guiding beliefs and assumptions lies at the heart of becoming a good leader. By providing structured feedback, promoting reflection, and developing self-awareness, we can create conditions in which reflective leaders flourish.

In his book *Reflective Practitioner* (1983), Donald Schön asks: What is the kind of knowing in which competent practitioners engage? How is professional knowing like and unlike the kinds of knowledge presented in academic textbooks, scientific papers, and learned journals? We can begin with the assumption that competent practitioners know more than they say, and that they exhibit a kind of knowing-in-practice, most of which is tacit. Reflection-in-action is central to the art by which leaders cope with the troublesomely divergent situations of practice. When practitioners reflect in action, they become researchers in the practice context.

Schön lets us in on his personal communications with academic leaders at Harvard and MIT: "The dean of a major school of management speaks of the inadequacy of established management theory and technique to deal with the increasingly critical task of managing complexity. The dean of a famous school of engineering observes that the nineteenth-century division of labor has become obsolete" (Schön 1983, 14). Times change, as do the constructs and skills needed to lead. Some of the major professions in universities are disciplined by an unambiguous end—health, law, sciences—and operate in stable institutional contexts. Chairs, on the other hand, are embroiled in conflicts of values, goals, purposes, and interests. Schön (1983) contends that it is reflection-in-action which is central to the "art" by which practitioners sometimes deal well with situations of uncertainty, instability, uniqueness, and value conflict.

For this reason alone, reflection-in-action is critically important. We must develop strategies for reflection that place technical problem-solving within a broader context of reflective inquiry. Chairs' isolation from one another works against reflection-in-action. Schön contends: "Managers do reflect-in-action, but they seldom reflect on their reflection-in-action. Hence this crucially important dimension of their art tends to remain private and inaccessible to others. Moreover, because awareness of one's intuitive thinking usually grows out of practice in articulating it to others, managers often have little access to their own reflection-in-action" (1983, 243). Chairs, then, need to communicate their private dilemmas and insights, to test them against the views of their peers. Leadership development does not take place in a vacuum (Beineke and Sublett 1999). It flourishes best within a group or with trusted colleagues who can act as mentors, partners, and coaches. Do you meet with your fellow chairs alone, without the dean present, to reflect and to support one another?

The development of leadership ability is a long and complex process. The influence of family, peers, education, sports, and social activities in high school and college impact individuals' ability to lead and their need for achievement, self-esteem, power, and service (Wolverton and Gmelch 2002). "If experience is such an important teacher, and the motivation to lead is rooted in one's past, and leadership skills are indeed so complex and related to one's work and past, what role can training hope to play?" (Conger 1992, 34).

Leadership development must incorporate all three approaches: conceptual development, skill building, and reflective practice (see chapter 8). Each integrates and builds upon the other. Nevertheless, development of leadership rests with individuals' own motivation and talent, and with the receptiveness of their organizations to supporting and coaching their skills. In part, leadership is passion, and you cannot teach people to be passionate.

## Chapter 2

Developing an Academic Team

In teamwork, silence isn't golden, it's deadly.
—Mark Sanborn

As faculty members become department chairs, they shift from being responsible for themselves as individuals to being responsible for the collective group or team, which we define as the department. Typically, an academic leader becomes less inner-directed and more other-directed, less an autonomous figure and more publicly accountable to others, less an authority in a disciplinary area and more an entrepreneur who must persuade, less a scholar immersed in research manuscripts and more a multi-skilled communications practitioner (Gmelch and Miskin 2004). Usually, a faculty member who becomes a chair moves from being a scholarly figure to an academic leader of department colleagues. The academic leader's challenge is to create a dynamic collective culture that bridges the differences of gender, race, ethnicity, and age to promote the development of a team.

Recent literature on leadership has identified the indispensability of teams and teamwork (Wergin 2003; Katzenbach and Smith 1993; Katzenbach 1998). Academic teams not only add value, they often foster respectful and enjoyable relationships. Department members may not always agree with one another, so an effective team process relies on mutual respect and the ability to "agree to disagree" while working productively together. The emergence of team culture depends chiefly on the department chair; it requires passion, commitment, and continual development.

Practitioners and scholars alike speak to the importance of fostering teamwork.

Some academic departments, like elite professional sports teams, behave like a *collection* of scholars, recruiting known stars in their disciplines, or very visibly lionizing their own stars. Such a department may be ranked nationally, but that does not guarantee that it is performing as synergistically as a championship team. Rather than hiring a collection of scholars with "hollowed collegiality," you would do better to envision your department as a *community* of scholars, whose thinking and actions turn from *my* work to *our* work, from self interests to public interests, from personal good to the common good. If your department meetings are prisoners to "administrivia" and individual turf wars, your unit may be well served by a change in culture, one in which you reshape the dialogue and gradually shift the emphasis to the common needs and interests of the department.

The following sections of this chapter will help you define what it means to be a team, assess your readiness to develop your department as a team, and investigate the key characteristics required for team building. As you read this chapter, reflect on the following questions to help you frame your investigation: Do you value each faculty member's contribution to your department's mission? What do you do to ensure that each member reaches his or her potential? How does the department as a whole support this value? How do you encourage individual creativity and how does that enhance the department's agenda? Do you encourage faculty to learn from and support each other in their professional activities? Do you reward collective behavior as well as individual performance? Do you and your colleagues hold each other to high standards of professional productivity? Have you collectively set direction and long range goals? Have you established common and acceptable behaviors and operating procedures?

DEFINITION OF ACADEMIC TEAMS

We have identified teams and team leadership as foundational to the development of a productive community of colleagues. But what, in practice, does that mean? Extensive literature exists on teams, team building, and team characteristics, much of which has been developed in the business world and in the volunteer sector. The definition provided here is adapted from Katzenbach and Smith and applied to academic teams (1993, 45). An academic team is *a manageable number of faculty members with multiple perspectives, complementary skills, and compatible group processes who are committed to a common purpose and hold themselves mutually accountable for its results.* Among the key elements of an academic team or department are its size, diversity, purpose(s), and commitment to accountability (Hecht, Higgerson, and Gmelch 1999). These are discussed below.

Size

What is the right size for a team? In higher education, academic departments range from a few faculty in small, discipline-specific departments to a few dozen in comprehensive departments (e.g., math and English) to hundreds in some professional schools. The average size of departments is somewhere between 16 and 18.6 members (McLaughlin, Malpass, and Montgomery 1975; Carroll 1990). In practice, smaller departments tend to be run by consensus while the larger departments (those larger than twenty-four) utilize multiple layers of decision making. The larger departments can, theoretically, constitute an academic team, but from a practical and operational standpoint, they are better suited for division into sub-academic or program teams. Much of the literature suggests that teams of eight to twelve perform most effectively, as the members are able to develop common purposes, common goals, collective operations, and mutual accountability. If the number falls too low, it becomes impossible to balance individual talents; if it rises too high, making decisions by consensus is impractical.

Diversity of perspectives and skills

Rather than build a team on personal compatibility, teams should have complementary and diverse perspectives in terms of discipline, experience, tenure, age, ethnicity, and gender. While diversity increases the challenge of team leadership, it creates opportunities for new ideas and team synergy.

Departments also need the right mix of technical, operational, analytical, problem-solving, and interpersonal skills. In both medium and large departments, you will have the latitude to structure teams that match tasks with talents and that balance skills and expertise—your role, in this case, is facilitator.

Agreement on common purposes

Faculty need to agree on how they will work together to accomplish their common purposes. When faculty approach a task—especially in an academic department—each has pre-existing professional assignments, as well as personal strengths, weaknesses, experience, talents, and perspectives. A department functioning as a work group becomes a team when faculty members realize that their own goals and successes are the best way for the department to achieve its goals and common purposes. While faculty members may not always agree, they must develop a social contract or common set of beliefs as to how they can work together. This raises the issue of individual goals in relation to team goals and emphasizes the importance of building team goals through the achievement of individual goals.

While it is important for academic leaders to set the directions and boundaries for a department or academic team, the team itself must have the flexibility to encourage support for common purposes. Faculty members often need a "rally point" to bring them together under a single banner, which can give impetus to their individual achievements.

Mutual accountability

The final element distinguishing an academic team from a group or collection of scholars is the necessity of holding itself accountable for its results. The subtle difference between "the leader holds faculty accountable" and "we, as faculty, hold ourselves accountable" is the difference between a group of faculty and an academic team. If your academic team is not committed to mutual accountability, then it will not likely be able to sustain itself around a common purpose.

In summary, academic teams don't just happen. Your department is certainly a group, but groups are not necessarily teams. Ask yourself the following questions regarding team elements:

1. Is your team the right size?

2. Are faculty skills diverse, yet complementary, and adequate to meet team needs?

3. Do team members share a common purpose and do their individual efforts support team goals?

4. Have faculty members agreed upon how they can work together to reach the common goal?

5. Will they hold themselves individually and mutually accountable to achieve the desired results?

STAGES OF TEAM DEVELOPMENT

Team literature describes the stages of development through which most teams pass. Tuckman articulates a four-stage process helpful in building a team (1955, 384-99). The assumption is that these stages unfold whenever a team is formed, but in fact, every time a new person joins a team the process may need to be revisited. Given the dynamic nature of academic teams, it is helpful to review the changing roles of chairs as the teams progress through these development stages, as shown in Figure 2.1.

1. *Forming.* In this stage, the group members identify the issues for which they will take responsibility, and get a sense of how they will work together. A department chair can stimulate a group to start forming a team through such activities as identifying courses, setting budget allocations, or even downsizing (creating motivation for the group to unify). The group must make tentative decisions about goals, membership, roles, and procedures. In this first stage, the academic leader assumes a more directive role by helping the group set the boundaries and standards of decision making. And as

Figure 2.1. Tuckman Model

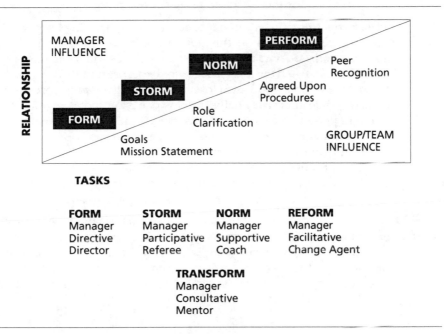

mentioned earlier, this metric may require attention whenever the makeup of faculty increases, decreases, or changes.

2. *Storming.* The group will undergo conflict as members react emotionally to the tasks at hand. Success in this stage is grounded in trust within the group. Academic leaders at this point do not want to suppress conflict, but to channel it in positive ways. Team leaders here become mediators or referees; they must be able to build trust by relating the goals of individual faculty members to departmental successes, and they must permit open discussions without introducing additional or unproductive conflict to the process.

3. *Norming.* Team members in the norming stage start to establish conscious standards for their work and agree on who will be responsible for which tasks (typically with the framework of research, teaching, and outreach). Dialogue becomes open and trust assumed. The fundamental change is that the group focuses on the issue or problem rather than the dynamics among its members. Conflict over goals, procedures, and roles during this cohesion stage will be resolved by sharing ideas and showing respect for one another's contributions. Unfortunately, some groups do not reach this stage, reverting instead to the protection of individual differ-

ences and interests. This is where the department chair must act as an assertive mediator or coach to bring the team together.

4. *Performing*. Here, the group concentrates on completing its tasks and resolving the issues. At this point, faculty members begin to function as an academic team. They resolve issues and begin to accept roles that match the team's needs for expertise and abilities. As members develop rapport and closeness, they will interact more informally. While informality helps develop cohesion and compatibility, it is important that it does not generate cliques or exclusive networks. Assuming that real teamwork has emerged, a sense of trust, informality, and cohesiveness may make it possible to exchange ideas and propose solutions via email, teleconferencing, and the like. The chair's role at this point in the development of a true academic team is that of consultant, mentor, and participant.

The "performing" stage is not the final step in team formation. There is another stage, "transforming," that continues as the team grows, develops, and loses or gains members. As noted in Figure 2.1, your role as leader becomes one of change-agent/facilitator as your team moves from one stage to another: you go from director (forming) to referee (storming) to coach (norming) to mentor (performing) to facilitator (transforming).

Barriers to Team Development

In introducing each stage of team development in your department, you may encounter structural, cultural, or political barriers. Often very complicated, these barriers seem inevitable in most academic settings and typically take the following forms:

- Academic departments tend to be discipline-driven, full of faculty whose individual interests do not cohere into a collective focus. Team culture does not require that diverse interests be subsumed, but it is important that they are able to complement and support one another.

- Faculty members traditionally receive credit toward tenure and promotion for their individual research or teaching efforts, rather than for overall department successes. You can encourage team culture to the degree that you can align individual faculty achievements with department goals.

- Turbulent and changing environments typically force an emphasis on short-term outcomes to the detriment of long-term goals. Team leaders recognize that just as faculty efforts support department achievements, department achievements must support college and institutional aims.

- Institutional goals are typically multiple, contradictory, unclear, and imposed on, rather than controlled by, faculty members.

- Stakeholders and constituents are pluralistic, unpredictable, and constantly changing, rather than singular and responsive to individual faculty members.

While these and other organizational barriers may not be easily remedied, academic leaders should anticipate and address them by developing effective team characteristics and a supportive team climate. A collective team attitude will enhance relationships and mitigate overly independent or even dysfunctional behaviors within the department.

RECOGNIZING AND ASSESSING TEAM CULTURE

Perhaps the best way to recognize team culture is to first understand what a team is not. Teams do not require all faculty members to meet every time a department decision needs to be made. Individual faculty members should not have identical interests and aspirations and they do not even need to agree with one another. Successful academic departments do not require homogeneous team players. In fact, it is the diversity of their concerns, ideas, and interests that contribute most to department success. Recognizing and encouraging the characteristics of collective team culture within your department can encourage individual achievement, improve department scholarship, and strengthen your faculty relationships.

The team-building literature is filled with descriptions and explanations of the required, necessary, or key characteristics of effectively functioning teams, which, when introduced to an organization, contribute significantly to the development of a supportive team culture. Dyer discusses five team-development phases (1977); Gmelch and Miskin present four principles for productive teams (2004); Larson and LaFasto identify eight properties of effectively functioning teams (1989); and Parker lists twelve team characteristics (1991). These and other team effectiveness studies may at first seem to confuse, rather than explain, how a department team is built. However, a critical review of the team literature reveals a common set of team attitudes or characteristics. Nearly all team studies agree that the collective team culture requires:

1. Clearly stated and agreed-upon long-term team goals.

2. Actively involved team members and shared management authority.

3. Openly shared information with participative decision making.

4. Constructive approaches to resolving conflict with attention to individual interests.

5. Top priority attention to individual growth and development.

Exercise 2.1. Assessing Department Team Culture

Review the comparison chart and for each characteristic, evaluate the status of your department by placing an "X" on the appropriate continuum below.

GOAL-ALIGNMENT:

Long-term direction shared with faculty and staff

Short-term department goals not aligned with individual goals

MANAGEMENT:

Shared with staff and faculty to utilize individual expertise

Power in position, held and delegated interaction

DECISION-MAKING:

Information available with open faculty interaction

Information restricted with limited faculty interaction

CONFLICT MANAGEMENT:

Collaborative solutions sought with emphasis on individual interests

Focus on problems with little attention to individual interests

FACULTY EXCELLENCE:

Emphasis on individual growth and development of individual faculty members

Emphasis on conformance to department standards rather than individuals

How to build these key characteristics in your department is not self-evident; the configuration of your faculty, the relationships among them, and their individual interests are unique to your department and merit your attention. As a start, however, assess the current relationship between each faculty member and the team culture you intend to cultivate by completing Exercise 2.1. The outcomes of the exercise will suggest areas upon which you might initially focus your attention.

BUILDING EFFECTIVE TEAM CHARACTERISTICS

Building each team characteristic can be a demanding experience. Table 2.1 suggests steps you can take to introduce each characteristic, setting those steps against typical expectations in "traditional" departments that undervalue team philosophies and practices.

We turn now to a discussion of how you might approach each team characteristic in your department.

Management

The key to effective team processes is a sharing of the management role. Faculty members have individual interests and must be encouraged to excel in them. You can view your management role as facilitating the achievements of your individual faculty members by making decisions that give meaning to their areas of expertise and that provide support for their efforts. As you build a supportive team that deals collaboratively with its problems, you will find that faculty differences (conflicts) become more manageable and productive. Carefully consider each conflict you encounter as you focus on fostering team culture.

Your management role is to encourage faculty achievements and support faculty goals that contribute to the department's success. Learning how to encourage individual faculty goals in relation to department goals is your best approach to influencing faculty.

Goal alignment

As mentioned earlier, department goals should support college and institutional successes. Just as importantly, faculty achievements should contribute to department successes. As a department chair, your role is to identify long-term, guiding, future department expectations and potentials. As the team leader, you must encourage individual faculty achievements that support the department— and, in the process, insist that the initiative for individual goals remain with the faculty members. You will need to informally and consistently share the overarching department goals with your faculty and inspire them to set their own challenges within the parameters of those goals.

Most of the faculty will be aware that the department has limited resources, and will certainly argue the merits of funding their particular initiatives. As team leader, you will need to seek ways to make individual faculty goals compatible with and supportive of department directions. In Table 2.2, we offer suggestions as to how individual faculty goals might be related to selected/possible department goals.

Focusing individual faculty goals toward team outcomes, as suggested by the examples in Table 2.2, is a critical element in the development of a department's team culture.

Table 2.1. Effective Team Characteristics

	COLLECTIVE TEAM ATTITUDE	TRADITIONAL DEPARTMENT CLIMATE
GOAL ALIGNMENT	• Long-term, future oriented goals • Established and modified to give the best possible match between individual goals and department goals • Commitment sought from all members of the department	• Short-term, changing, operational goals • Little consideration given to individual or personal goals • Imposed upon the group by the chair
MANAGEMENT	• A shared responsibility • All faculty members feel responsible for contributing to the department goals • Different members, because of their knowledge or abilities, act as "resource expert" at different times, thus the management roles change as the tasks of the department change	• Delegated by position • Position determines influence • Obedience to authority the accepted norm • Power concentrated in authority positions
DECISION MAKING	• Information openly shared with all staff and faculty • Decisions reached by consensus • All members usually in agreement with final results or outcomes, after all interested parties have been heard and understood • Disagreements usually constructive to each common understanding and improve conceptual acceptance	• Information restricted or unavailable • Decisions made by authority • Those in opposition expected to "go along," even though in actual practice they often remain resentful
CONFLICT MANAGEMENT	• Conflict and controversy viewed as positive and essential to the problem-solving process • Disagreements may be frequent and candid, but relatively comfortable • Little evidence of personal attack: criticism is constructive and even supportive in nature • Interests of all parties explored with collaborative search for common solution	• Conflict viewed as destructive barrier to problem solving and is consciously ignored or suppressed • Disagreements may be suppressed by the chair or "resolved" by a majority vote, which leaves a still unconvinced minority • Criticism is embarrassing and produces tension, often leading to accommodation or compromise • Emphasis on department position with little attention to the interests of conflicting parties

Table 2.2   Relationship between Department and Individual Faculty Goals

1. DEPARTMENT GOAL: DISTINCTION IN FACULTY EXCELLENCE
Possible goals for individual faculty members:
- manuscript accepted for publication from the department's list of desired journals
- revise and resubmit — acceptance at the top level of the desired-journals list
- regional or national recognition for a discipline-specific scholarly participation/achievement
- committee or chair position on scholarly advisory board or with recognized field agency
- identified research stream or research partnership with an academic colleague

2. DEPARTMENT GOAL: STUDENTS AS CLIENTS AND COLLEAGUES
Possible goals for individual faculty members:
- identified innovation or significant revision within current teaching assignment
- development of new courses or academic programs
- increased interactions between students and constituent communities
- revised presence of projects, papers, or journal requirements in pedagogy
- active participation of students in publishable research projects

3. DEPARTMENT GOAL: EXCELLENCE IN PROGRAM DESIGN AND DELIVERY
Possible goals for individual faculty members:
- serve on college undergraduate-curriculum committee
- take the lead of the department degree-revision committee
- oversee department internship and certificate programs
- serve as advisor to student club
- develop new program proposal for faculty review and preparation for university approval

4. DEPARTMENT GOAL: OUTREACH AND SERVICE TO CONSTITUENCIES
Possible goals for individual faculty members:
- participate in an approved partnership with a selected constituent or agency
- support department development campaign
- develop and complete a specific plan for individual improvement and growth this year
- establish active relationships with selected department constituents

Decision making

A team-oriented decision process is needed to inspire and unite faculty effort and direction. As team leader you should first establish an open climate of shared information. While it is not practical (or necessary) to send all information to all faculty members at all times, you do want an environment where faculty members are willing to ask for and expect to receive information they consider important. Second, take time to consciously and consistently build understanding among faculty. Create acceptance for organizational decisions by sharing team goals and successes with all faculty as frequently as you can. This does not require that a meeting be held for every decision made, only that faculty trust you to inform them, consult them, and allow them to influence decisions whenever pertinent to their interests.

Open and frequent discussions with your faculty concerning their individual achievements, challenges, and plans are both desirable and necessary. Such discussions encourage more productive relationships. The team decision-making process is more participative than directive. It may not be quick or easy, and will require your emotional commitment, your competence, and your confidence. As team leader, your role is to inspire enthusiasm, invite commitment, and add enjoyment to the process. Facilitating team culture among faculty colleagues remains your responsibility and will require your passion.

Conflict management

Conflict, controversy, and disagreement are to be expected—perhaps even valued—but must not be allowed to render the team dysfunctional (see chapter 6). Explore the interests of your faculty and strive to satisfy their needs through collaborative solutions. Encourage this climate informally, consistently, and among all individuals in your unit. We suggested earlier that individual faculty members prefer to set their own directions and goals, and should be encouraged to do so. Your leadership role in this process is not to develop annual goals for faculty members, but to share a vision of the future with them that will encourage, excite, or inspire development of their goals in line with department interests and priorities. Be prepared to openly discuss department concerns and priorities with your faculty members. These discussions can encourage more productive and more enjoyable relationships; ultimately, they will allow you to do four things: 1) reduce dysfunctional conflict, 2) encourage individual faculty excellence, 3) connect individual achievements to department goals, and 4) recognize the individual achievements of each faculty member.

Faculty excellence

Underlying the issue of dysfunctional conflict is the importance of each faculty member. As you know, department success depends absolutely on capable, willing, and competent faculty members. As team leader, your priority may not be the reduction of conflict, but the development and success of each individual faculty member. Team leaders encourage faculty members—who have discipline-specific interests, skills, abilities, needs, and professional goals—to link their individual efforts and aspirations to department success.

For example, you can influence faculty choices as you discuss and negotiate individual goals and budget allocations for the coming year. For those faculty members who are doing well in both setting and meeting their goals, additional attention may not be necessary. Encourage these faculty members through public recognition, appropriate feedback, and generous budget support. Other faculty members may need a more structured approach. Much evidence indicates that "individual action-planning," characterized by goal setting and the establishment of specific, sequential activities with target dates, can be beneficial (Gmelch and Miskin 2004; Thompson, Strickland, and Gamble 2005). A sample of an individual planning form is shown in Figure 2.2.

34

Figure 2.2. Action Planning Form

SPECIFY THE INDIVIDUAL GOAL:

LIST THE ACTION STEPS (IN SEQUENTIAL ORDER) THAT YOU BELIEVE WILL BE NEEDED TO ACCOMPLISH THIS GOAL:

Specific Action Step	Planned Completion Date	Person Accountable For This Step
1.		
2.		
3.		
4.		
5.		
6.		
7.		
8.		

An effective individual planning process can:

1. *Prompt initiative and impetus.* That is, help inexperienced or reluctant faculty members identify a beginning point on new or complicated projects. For example, faculty members who want to redirect their research focus, but have not yet begun the process, can use this process to bring excitement as new research streams are developed.

2. *Define approach, steps, and sequence.* In individual planning, a faculty member determines the specific steps, proper sequence, and

appropriate time frame for accomplishing a goal, identifying who is accountable for the completion of each step along the way. For example, newer faculty members determined to upgrade their teaching ratings might identify alternative instructional methodologies, propose mentorship options, request collegial reviews, and clarify possible curricular changes.

3. *Ensure coordination.* Faculty goals, even when aligned with team priorities, are seldom accomplished without the involvement of other people in or outside the department. For example, a new program to involve students in applied industry-related projects will require organization and coordination. General/informal agreements between faculty are desirable starting points, but are frequently forgotten or even withdrawn as other activities emerge throughout the year. The individual faculty plan, prepared in cooperation with other colleagues or sponsors, can help ensure that early efforts at organization remain sturdy.

4. *Foster innovation.* Individual plans may prompt faculty members to solicit suggestions on how to reach difficult goals or to seek new ideas for approaching old problems. Individuals who are usually averse to criticism or suggestions from others may be open to input when it comes to implementing their own planned initiatives.

5. *Promote communication.* Individual action planning encourages faculty members to communicate progress toward goals that may be difficult to evaluate. For instance, a faculty goal to initiate a new research stream may need some method of interim reporting, and if the new stream will not bring publications for a year or two, it may frustrate individuals when the annual feedback is less than expected. Faculty members can use their individual plans to report specific and significant progress in each step completed even when no final goals have been reached. This valuable role in the appraisal process should not be underestimated.

The essence of academic leadership lies in the ability to develop a functioning *community of faculty colleagues who work as a team*. Like any leadership task, team building is an ongoing process. The faculty-focused team leadership model discussed here identifies the continuing development of faculty members as your first priority and offers a more productive approach to department success.

Team leadership is an *influencing process* (Miskin and Gmelch 1985). Regardless of whether you promote the achievement of team or individual faculty goals, the team approach entails continual encouragement of individual faculty effort, excitement, and achievement. Developing individual faculty members and supporting their achievements is not only a priority in achieving department goals, but comes with an enjoyable side benefit: it improves the climate among faculty and brings a bit of fun into the department. Listen carefully as you provide overall team direction. Encourage, recognize, celebrate, and reward individual faculty achievements. Identify and communicate your team's goals. Use your judgment, imagination, and team-leadership skills to encourage team culture as you build individual faculty excellence.

Chapter 3

ENCOURAGING DEPARTMENT PRODUCTIVITY

Which way did they go?
How many were there?
I must find them.
I am their leader.
— Anonymous

Is your department defining its own directions, or are your decisions really controlled by pressures from administrators, external stakeholders, relevant constituents, and faculty? When the dean announces a drive for increased enrollments, but denies your request for an additional faculty line, what freedom do you have to assign faculty workloads? When student enrollments increase dramatically in one area, but dwindle in another, what flexibility do you have to guide curriculum emphasis? When your advisory board withdraws support for regional fund raising and suggests increasing extramural grant funding, how can you direct the outcomes for your development campaigns? When faculty members in one discipline initiate new courses or programs, is it too late to influence department direction?

In most cases, department productivity doesn't just happen. Quality leadership is the necessary catalyst, which is why the position of "department chair" exists. Chairs not only make decisions, but, more importantly, determine what decisions need to be made.

Leading a department involves, from the outset, three questions:

1. What opportunities/potentials are out there for the department? (Department Analysis)

39

2. What are the current levels of department productivity, and how can they be continued/improved? (Department Planning)

3. How can the chair influence faculty productivity? (Implementation)

Whether new to the chair position or a seasoned veteran faced with new and changing conditions, you need to know as much as possible about the various environs in which your department operates. Departments do not exist in isolated lab settings; they are functioning units in educational institutions and are continuously impacted by interactions with students, parents, future employers, faculty, and all other stakeholders. In a way, each of these constitutes an environment in which your department must live sustainably. Data from your surroundings is thus the lifeblood of your department's future. Gathering these data require continuous effort; analyzing them is an integral part of your leadership process (see Figure 3.1).

DEPARTMENT ANALYSIS: WHAT ARE THE POTENTIAL OPPORTUNITIES?

Your broader external environments

Educational institutions do not operate as traditional hierarchies. They are however, influenced by many of the same forces as the community, nation, and world at large. National and international politics, technological advances, and economic fluctuations present both threats to and opportunities for your department's future.

To gain insight from your external environments, systematically consider the following questions:

- How might current economic projections impact your enrollments, budgets, and faculty recruiting?
- Do you anticipate significant changes in current student enrollments, faculty availability, and stakeholder interests?
- What broad social trends do you anticipate and what is their significance to your department?
- How might new technological developments influence your department?
- Does any new legislation have the potential to affect your department?
- What values held by your stakeholders are important to the planning process?

Figure 3.1 Department Leadership Model: Department Analysis

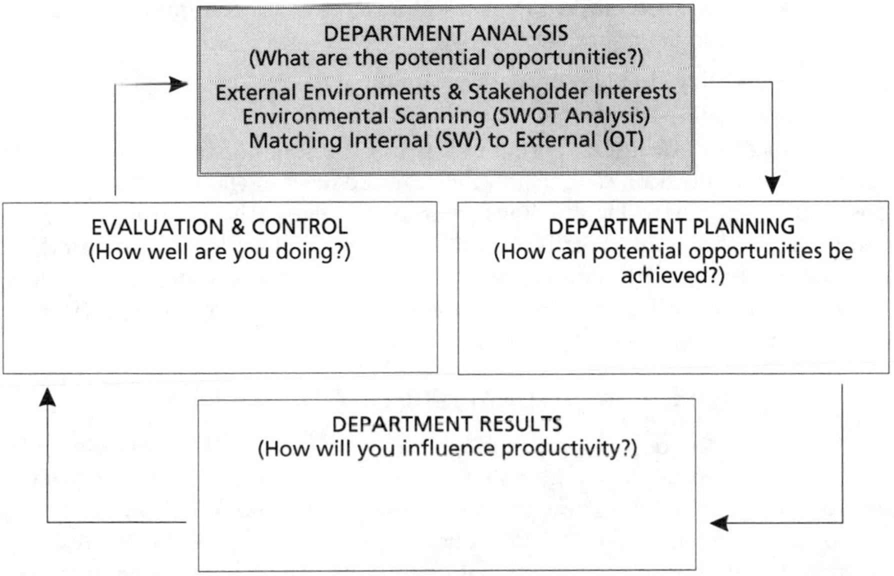

DEPARTMENT ANALYSIS
(What are the potential opportunities?)

External Environments & Stakeholder Interests
Environmental Scanning (SWOT Analysis)
Matching Internal (SW) to External (OT)

EVALUATION & CONTROL
(How well are you doing?)

DEPARTMENT PLANNING
(How can potential opportunities be achieved?)

DEPARTMENT RESULTS
(How will you influence productivity?)

- Which areas of teaching specialization are gaining prominence locally, regionally, or nationally?
- What are the trends or new developments in your discipline and academic fields?
- What are other institutions similar to yours doing that has relevance to your planning?

Stakeholder interests

The importance of serving stakeholders is universally accepted, but who are they? Currently-enrolled students are certainly stakeholders; their future employers also hold a stake in your decisions. Additionally, users of discipline expertise, potential new students, department alums, and the larger community all deserve attention. Not only can students, potential employers, and other department stakeholders suggest directions and trends, but they often provide innovative ideas for new programs, systems, or delivery methods. Identify who your department serves and seek data to clarify their interests by systematically addressing each of them. Here are a few sample questions:

- Can your students be described using identifiable groupings?
- What are their specific interests and concerns?
- What do you know about the placement of your graduates?

- What value are you offering to potential students? How is this perceived by them and their future employers?
- Which constituent groups are relevant to your community, discipline, and alumni relationships?
- What values held by other department stakeholders are relevant to your planning process?

The signal of declining enrollment is not the time to start learning about your student population. The search for qualified teaching faculty should not be postponed until new faculty lines become available. Fund-raising projects should not be the only impetus for building alumni relationships. Encouraging specific research activity should lead, rather than follow, your department decisions. The present is the best time to anticipate relevant change and prepare for the changing conditions of the future.

Environmental scanning (SWOT analysis)

Analyzing the department requires awareness of relevant environments. This awareness allows you to identify the *opportunities and threats* (OT) of the future, then use your department's *strengths and weaknesses* (SW) to address them. The acronym "SWOT" represents the essence of department analysis. While you can't control your external conditions, you can direct your department's resources in accordance with your changing environments.

Such introspective evaluation allows you to prevent or reduce anticipated threats from external environments. However, the preeminent value of this analysis lies in its ability to recognize and seize opportunities (Alfred et al. 2006; Barney and Arikan, 2001; Bridges and Mitchell, 2000; Eckel, Green, and Hill 2001; Hax and Majluf 1991; Morrill 2007; Priem and Butler 2001; Trainer 2004). Finding the time for frequent, formal analyses of your department's environments may not be possible on a regular basis, but understanding the process will prove highly useful. Always be alert for possible threats and potential opportunities in your external environments—and then manage your department's strengths to meet those challenges.

1. *External opportunities and threats.* Changes in economic conditions, student enrollments, and employer or community interests are outside your control and may pose threats to your department's success from time to time. Identifying threats from areas like these can help obviate problems. But for a leader, what is more important than foreseeing problems is recognizing opportunities. Opportunities can be found in almost every environmental change, and are often just the flip side of threats. An example from real life is a department that faced changes in its national accreditation requirements; the changes were initially viewed as threats to already deficient resources. But the changes also permitted the department

to realign and combine two existing programs, an opportunity that might have gone unnoticed had the chair not been poised to seek opportunities in external forces.

2. *Internal strengths and weaknesses.* The forces surrounding your department will impact its future, but it's the internal processes that are under your leadership control. Weaknesses in your department will hamper its ability to meet collective goals and respond to shifting environments. As you prepare to consider areas of your department that need improvement, consider questions like these:

- Do you see specific patterns of declining enrollments?
- Are there particular faculty members that consistently receive poor teaching evaluations?
- Do some individual research streams fail to support the department's overall interests?
- Can you identify any individual faculty members who are dysfunctional in terms of the overall department?
- Is your time consumed by unproductive advisory board (or other) meetings?

Your answers to these and similar questions will lead to initiating improvement efforts, realigning resources, or even discontinuing unproductive activities.

To address your department's weaknesses, you need to understand its strengths—positive abilities and situations within the department, college, or university that enable your department to take advantage of changes in its external environments. What is your department doing particularly well? How strong is your department's team climate? The following sample questions can give insight into this process:

- How open, collaborative, and supportive are your departmental relationships?
- What are the specific strengths of your individual faculty?
- Which teaching areas are achieving notable enrollments, learning, or placement?
- Which current research streams have or promise to have national prominence?
- Which constituents currently provide strong department support?
- What are the best opportunities for attracting additional resources?

In short, anything productive your department has that can be continued, strengthened, or built upon should be identified as an internal strength.

Matching strengths to opportunities

Ameliorating department weaknesses is important to your resource allocation decisions, but look to department strengths as your vital link to department success. As department chair, you need to use the interests and teaching abilities of your most effective faculty members to guide program development. Tie the most prominent research-interests of your faculty to your department's long-term goals. Build on existing student quality to develop department relationships with future employers. Utilize your best professional contacts to direct the department's commitment to community partnerships.

Exercise 3.1 will help you analyze your department's processes and plan how to take advantage of opportunities using your department's strengths. Gather your data informally, but with conscious intent. This sort of analysis will sharpen the focus of your planning.

DEPARTMENT PLANNING: HOW CAN POTENTIAL OPPORTUNITIES BE REALIZED?

"Planning for the future is important, and I'll get to it just as soon as I get past these current crises." "Inspiring faculty to greater achievement would be a welcome challenge if I didn't have to spend so much time on the little things." "It's so difficult to re-allocate budgets when I have to deal with protective faculty attitudes." "Meetings, schedules, and deadlines typically preempt my attention to any long-range planning." These expressions, from experienced and new chairs alike, reflect the frustrations often encountered in managing an academic department. Your challenge is to find a way to attend to these day-to-day department activities while providing the leadership so critical to your department's future. Or, more correctly, your challenge is to provide the leadership so critical to your department's future *through* these day-to-day management requirements. Figure 3.2 gives emphasis to the planning element of the department leadership model.

Creating the department's vision/mission

During a recent search for a new department chair, the dean of a college was asked, "What will be your expectations of the new chair?" The dean replied, "The chair will be expected to move this department into its proper future." The dean explained that the real challenge of a chair is to be aware of the department's past, present, and future surroundings, and to provide the kind of vision and focus that inspire faculty and staff.

This answer clearly identifies the leadership role of the chair position. While the dean's answer included typical attention to scheduling, student learning, faculty involvement, public visibility, etc., the main focus was on the lead-

Exercise 3.1. Department Analysis

You should conduct this analysis at your initiative. It can be informal and voluntary, but must include input, critique, and feedback from all relevant stakeholders (faculty, staff, students, dean, constituent groups, etc.).

I. Anticipated Opportunities	II. Department Strengths	III. Recommendations for acting on opportunities
From anticipated changes in your broader external environments:		
1.	1.	1.
2.	2.	2.
3.	3.	3.
4.	4.	4.
From recognized student, employer, community, and other stakeholder interests:		
1.	1.	1.
2.	2.	2.
3.	3.	3.
4.	4.	4.

ership requirement. This concept is given additional clarity in John Diebold's description of vision:

> Humans need purpose—individually and collectively. Without a sense of purpose, the individual is not only lost, but will rapidly disintegrate. Without purpose there is no motivation, no direction, no way to focus the physical and mental faculties of the human. What is true of the individual is even more true of the collective—be it the tribe, the nation, the corporation, the union. What holds the body politic together is the communality of purpose.
>
> When we say "vision," however, we mean more than a commitment to do now what must be done now. Vision implies a purpose beyond the moment, a view of the future, a dreaming and thinking ahead. A vision suggests the imaginative conceptualization of a future that is not inconsistent with the present, but that will move the present to something nearer to the ideal. (1984, 401)

What is your role in providing the department with a vision? One view is that leaders must first create the vision and then persuade others to follow (Bass 1985). An alternative view is that leaders discover a vision that is already present

Figure 3.2 Department Leadership Model: Department Planning

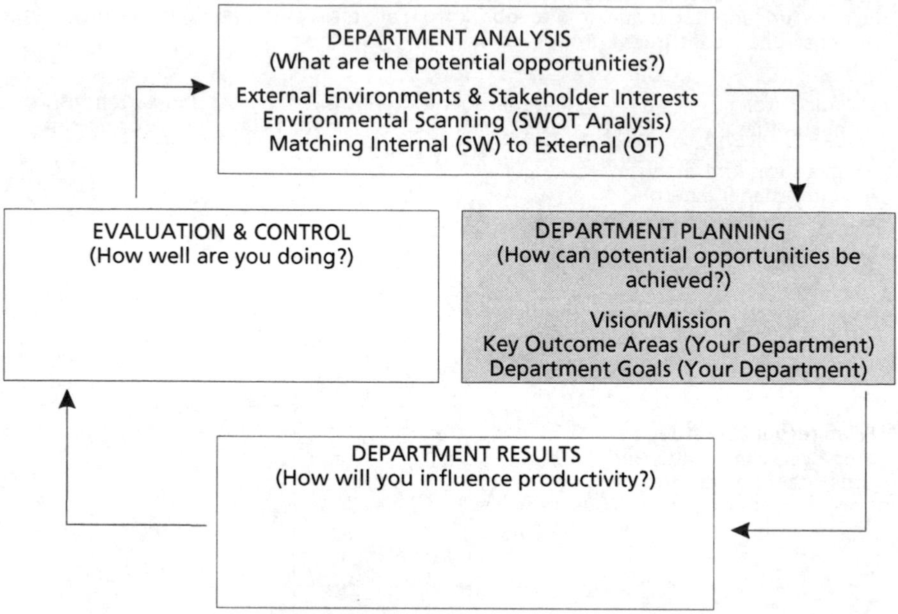

DEPARTMENT ANALYSIS
(What are the potential opportunities?)

External Environments & Stakeholder Interests
Environmental Scanning (SWOT Analysis)
Matching Internal (SW) to External (OT)

EVALUATION & CONTROL
(How well are you doing?)

DEPARTMENT PLANNING
(How can potential opportunities be achieved?)

Vision/Mission
Key Outcome Areas (Your Department)
Department Goals (Your Department)

DEPARTMENT RESULTS
(How will you influence productivity?)

among their constituents and give it articulation (Cleveland 1985). Other authors suggest that both views are correct. Vision is more powerfully shared when inspired by the strong personal conviction and motivation of a department leader. And vision becomes richer as it emanates from a variety of faculty, clientele, and external sources relevant to the department (Aldag and Joseph 2000; Bligh and Mendl 2005; Bowman 2002; Diamond 2002; Dooris 2002/2003; Nanus 1992; Shaw 2006).

Creating or articulating a department's vision requires frequent, consistent communication. A compelling commitment to a planned future cannot be achieved casually or intermittently. Your department's vision need not be couched in sophisticated rhetoric or presented in perfect strategic format. To be meaningful, what it needs is to send a continuous, consistent message concerning the following four elements:

1. *Visual conceptualization.* Effective department chairs build a picture of what the end result (potential future) will look like. You may not know exactly how you are going to get there, but you do need a clear idea of what the department is striving for. Can you create a visual conceptualization of your department's future? How can you best share that with your faculty? Can you help your faculty "feel" or

"see" this potential and how they fit into it? Can you share these images of long-term potential with all stakeholders?

2. *Future orientation.* Over and above organizing tasks, setting goals, and meeting short-term deadlines, a department chair needs to be preoccupied with the future. Staff and faculty typically (and appropriately) operate more in the here and now. Department leadership, on the other hand, must adopt a future-oriented framework that can unite these daily activities and decisions.

   While faculty teaching loads and course assignments must be determined each semester, the need to improve teaching effectiveness tends to require a two- or three-year planning transition. Individual faculty research must be encouraged continuously, but a shift in department research-paradigms will require three to five years of preparation and planning. Class size and number of sections are immediate concerns, but anticipating the interests of future students and potential employers calls for planning with a longer scope.

3. *Unique focus.* It is your role as department chair to provide meaningful focus to all activities and decisions. Can you develop a department mission statement that will communicate a perspective singular to your department's potential? While a vision/mission statement must, by definition, be visual and future-oriented, it must also be particular to your department. It should encourage your staff to capitalize on specific department strengths and take advantage of opportunities in your external environments. Take a look at how your department's vision/mission is articulated: how well does it distinguish between the specific potentials of the department and the overall framework of the institution?

4. *Inspiration.* Operational goals achieve short-term results (what is planned), rather than long-term visions (what we dream about). Vision/mission statements are designed to inspire creative and exciting short-term accomplishments. They identify alternatives, possibilities, ideals, and expressions of hope. Carefully review your department's vision/mission statement. Is it in writing? Does it exude a sense of potential, a plan for the future, a standard of excellence?

Building a vision/mission statement

Instead of worrying about the terminology of "vision" and "mission," trying to differentiate between vision-purposes and mission-purposes, build your statement around defining and encouraging potential. Does your vision/mission statement provide a shift from the organizational to the inspirational? As you prepare to write or revise one for your department, keep the following recommendations in mind:

- Be sure it is in a format that can be shared openly and easily
- Design it to include each of the above vision-elements (visual, future-oriented, unique, inspiring)
- Make sure it is simple, understandable, and available to all department personnel.

Consider this statement, generated by a mid-sized department in education: The mission of the Department of Educational Administration is to establish distinctive academic programs and encourage nationally recognized faculty to best meet the needs of our educational community.

Though broad, this mission statement sends a strong signal to faculty and staff regarding the priorities, strategies, and directions that should guide their short-term activities and decisions. While it is brief and easy to read, it clearly establishes four priorities: 1) high-quality (distinctive) academic programs, 2) nationally recognized faculty scholarship, 3) highest-quality graduates, and 4) relationships with the educational community.

This example is not intended to suggest appropriate or best priorities for all academic departments. It is, however, a good example of setting long-term guiding principles. Recall the analysis of environments from earlier in the chapter and review the strengths and priorities identified in Exercise 3.1. Now, get your department's stakeholders actively involved in this process by having them review your first draft of your vision/mission statement. You can use Exercise 3.2 to assist you in this process.

Key outcome areas

Your vision/mission statement describes the long-term intentions of the department. It sets the priorities for all department efforts. To be most useful, it has to be more than a broad picture of the future. Identifying specific areas in which results are vital to department success—which entails defining what success in those areas will look like (key outcomes)—is a vital but oft-neglected element of department unity. Key outcome areas common to academic departments are suggested in the literature; they are summarized in Table 3.1 (Bare 1980; Coleman 2004; Creswell et al. 1990; Huffman 2002; Leaming 2003).

When you identify the five or six key outcomes critical to your department's mission, you can create a cohesive meaning for your many department activities. Those activities, absent the structure of key outcomes, can become quite unfocused. You will get a sense of this from Table 3.2, a chair's list of the administrative duties she performed during a single week. The list is cumbersome, and it's obvious that without clear articulation, a chair's vision can be obscured by the many facets of day-to-day decision-making.

If this same chair, using information from her department analysis, organized the many activities listed above into five key outcome areas, it would look something like Table 3.3. Table 3.3 comprises the same activities as Table 3.2.

Exercise 3.2 Mission Statement Worksheet

Identify your department's scope and potential based on your previous analysis of the opportunities and challenges of your changing environments. This can be assisted by answering the following questions:

---

1. What changes do you anticipate in the students who will, in the future, be served by your department?

---

2. What changes do you believe are possible from department faculty members?

---

3. What changes do you anticipate among relevant stakeholder interests (external constituencies)?

---

4. What opportunities can you envision from other department resources and challenges?

With these opportunities and priorities in mind, prepare a brief, to-the-point narrative statement that communicates the *excitement and future-orientation* of the vision/mission for your department.

Vision/Mission Statement

However, it is more organized and adds focus and purpose to every activity. It identifies areas critical to the department and places everyone's daily activities in a future-oriented context.

Key outcomes from your vision/mission statement

Developing a set of key outcome areas for your department can provide organization and direction not only for you, but for your faculty as well. Take some time now to list the key outcome areas for your department and prepare specific descriptions for each. (Remember, the key outcome areas common to most academic departments are discussed in Table 3.1.) These will represent the priorities for your faculty and staff. They will explain the mission statement to all interested parties, enhance long-term direction, and provide contextual meaning. What better way to make decisions about priorities, time, and budgets? What better process for encouraging daily activity toward longer-term department goals? Once this step is complete, you can focus on directing daily

---

Table 3.1 Key Outcomes Common to Academic Departments

STUDENT LEARNING
- national scores
- student evaluations
- skill development
- degree completion
- placement data
- alumni relations
- other notable student achievement

FACULTY ACHIEVEMENT
- research activity
- research results
- teaching methodology
- teaching effectiveness
- university service
- community service

CONSTITUENT RELATIONS
- potential employers
- student groups
- professional organizations
- community organizations
- state government agencies
- federal government agencies

ACADEMIC PROCESS
- budget information
- budget allocation
- planning system
- student-records system
- academic program review
- personnel evaluation and review

DEPARTMENT RESOURCES
- effective utilization of current resources
- additional support from the dean
- community partnership programs
- extramural grant funding
- private development funds

---

functions, decisions, and activities toward the desired department results (key outcomes).

Let us review the earlier example of the department chair's vision/mission statement:

The mission of the Department of Educational Administration is to establish distinctive academic programs and encourage nationally recognized faculty scholarship. This department's main purpose is to prepare quality student graduates to best meet the needs of our educational community.

Table 3.2 Chair Activities

The following are a department chair's administrative duties, recorded in order of their performance during one week:

• schedule classes • seek opportunities to recognize constituent groups • make service-committee assignments • establish department standards • review and monitor student achievement • make regular field visits to important constituents • assess employer satisfaction with our graduates • improve lab facilities • establish acceptance of diversity among faculty • encourage student participation in programs • involve faculty in department goals • coordinate summer-school assignments • generate development-funding sources • seek additional budget resources • compare national scores and results • build a cooperative spirit among faculty • allocate limited resources • select advisory committees	• invite relevant stakeholders to make campus visits • approve student course requests • call and conduct faculty meetings • set curricular standards • support student organizations • hire quality department staff • invite new class offerings • interact regularly with advisory committees • establish department goals • handle student discipline problems • assign equitable teaching loads • submit annual budget • provide feedback to faculty • require job descriptions for all positions • encourage effective classroom learning • provide adequate research support to faculty • monitor enrollments • submit faculty salary recommendations • counsel students • advise and counsel faculty

This vision/mission is made more specific, more directive, and more usable by adding the department's key outcomes:

We, the faculty and staff of the Department of Educational Administration, earnestly and consistently strive for:

• PRIORITY FOCUS ON STUDENTS AS CLIENTS AND COLLEAGUES

Student achievement is realized only through a partner relationship and a supportive, collaborative involvement with faculty.

Student graduates will be recognized by the educational community, state constituencies, and alumni groups as being of the highest quality in the state.

• DISTINCTION IN RESEARCH AND SCHOLARSHIP

Distinction among faculty and students in their research and scholarship is a measure of the department's ability to compete at the university and national levels.

Table 3.3 Chair Activities within your Key Outcome Areas

STUDENT LEARNING
- encourage effective classroom learning
- review and monitor student achievement
- assess employer satisfaction with our graduates
- encourage student participation in programs
- counsel students
- handle student discipline problems
- support student organizations
- compare national scores and results

FACULTY ACHIEVEMENT
- establish acceptance of diversity among faculty
- build a cooperative spirit among faculty
- involve faculty in department goals
- provide adequate research-support to faculty
- call and conduct faculty meetings
- provide feedback to faculty
- assign equitable teaching loads
- make service-committee assignments
- advise and counsel faculty
- submit faculty salary recommendations

CONSTITUENT RELATIONS
- select advisory committees
- interact regularly with advisory committees
- make regular field visits to important constituents
- invite relevant stakeholders to make campus visits
- seek opportunities to recognize constituent groups

ACADEMIC PROCESS
- establish department standards
- establish department goals
- invite new class offerings
- seek additional budget resources
- require job descriptions for all positions
- approve student course requests
- coordinate summer-school assignments
- schedule classes
- monitor enrollments

DEPARTMENT RESOURCES
- allocate limited resources
- submit annual budget
- set curricular standards
- improve lab facilities
- generate development-funding sources

Collectively, the faculty will present a portfolio of national scholarship, professional activity, and collegial efforts.

- DISTINCTION IN SERVICE TO THE EDUCATIONAL COMMUNITY

In order to distinguish the department as a powerful service-provider, staff and faculty must be visible and recognized as contributing members of our educational community.

- EXCELLENCE IN PROGRAM DESIGN AND DELIVERY

Selective offerings of academic programs will reflect the opportunities of our educational community and the strengths of our department.

A fundamental purpose of this department is to achieve recognized excellence in the design and delivery of all offered academic programs.

- ENLARGEMENT OF RESOURCES FOR DEPARTMENT SUPPORT

Since excellence is worth the cost, the acquisition of sufficient professional resources within the department is essential to our success.

Professional grants, constituent support, student funding, and university development activities are valued and encouraged by the department.

This completes the vision/mission and makes it easy to visualize this department's future challenges. Notice how the long-term commitment to excellence in each of the major areas is not only listed, but explained and given emphasis. This allows the chair, staff, and faculty to keep their day-to-day discussions, activities, decisions, and goals focused on key outcomes—rather than on a long, fragmented list of responsibilities.

Drawing on your earlier and ongoing analyses, use Exercise 3.3 to identify and describe the key outcomes critical to your department's future. Identifying and paying specific attention to department strengths will give you insight into the priorities (outcomes) unique to your department and its external environments.

You now have the framework for future discussions and decisions with your faculty and staff. When communicated openly and properly, these key outcome areas should direct all effort and decision. Even so, don't get too caught up in the process of writing the perfect vision/mission statement. Be aware that neither format nor wording is the most important issue here. Informal, but consistent, communications can be just as effective (if not more so). The critical issue is to develop a vision/mission and for which you interpret the key outcome areas as clearly as possible. This requires significant input from staff, faculty, relevant stakeholders, and, of course, the dean. Be certain that your university, your college, your department, and your constituents value achievement in each of the key outcome areas you've identified. Once developed, it must be

---

Exercise 3.3 Key Outcomes Worksheet

Using your mission statement from Exercise 3.2, list the four or five key outcome areas critical to your department. Consider only major areas that, if neglected, will be detrimental to the department's future.

---

1. Student-related:

---

2. Faculty-related:

---

3. Constituencies:

---

4. Other:

---

5. Other:

With these specific areas in mind, prepare brief narrative statements to detail your department's commitment to excellence for each key outcome.

Key outcome 1

Key outcome 2

Key outcome 3

Key outcome 4

Key outcome 5

---

shared. Post it in the department, distribute it to clients, publish it in the newsletter, initiate a series of memos, include it in your department correspondence. Figure 3.2 shows an actual letter from one chair's attempt to share her department's long-term aspirations (mission and key outcome areas).

The effectiveness of your communications will not be measured by formality or by method of distribution. What will make them most useful are consistency and frequency. When developed collectively (and this takes time), clarified in written form (whatever the medium), and openly shared (whatever your

---

Figure 3.2 Memorandum

Copy of a memo from a department chair who was experiencing a lack of team attitude among faculty.

MEMO

TO: Department Faculty
FROM: Department Chair
SUBJECT: Next faculty meeting

In our last faculty meeting, four areas were identified for attention. I would like to detail some specific suggestions under each area. At the upcoming faculty meeting, I would like to discuss: 1) if you all agree that these four foci are appropriate, and 2) if so, do you agree with the suggestions I have offered under each category. I am also interested if you have any additional suggestions. Here goes:

1. INTEGRATION OF THE DEPARTMENT

We need to think and function as one department. I perceive this objective as a pre-requisite to departmental survival. To this aim, I recommend:

- The whole department, not areas within the department, decide on doctoral student admission. Admission of all new doctoral students, beginning immediately, should be considered in light of departmental needs—not any one area's needs. We will have an opportunity at the next faculty meeting to recruit doctoral students with departmental welfare in mind.

- Recruitment of new faculty should similarly be viewed as a decision to benefit the whole department and not pit factions within the department against each other. We need to carefully select candidates who can meet the department's research, teaching, and service expectations as well as meet the needs of our external constituencies.

2. RESPONSIVE TO STAKEHOLDER NEEDS

We need to be attentive to our environment and major stakeholders within it (students, alumni, industry, administration). Towards this aim, I propose:

- We need major revision in our curriculum (courses offered, content of the courses, and teaching methodology). We can start this effort with input from our focus groups. We need to get rid of useless courses, be more flexible in teaching methods (e.g., have students do real-life projects and use team-teaching), and draw in more students to our classes rather than require them to take our classes.

- We need to be responsive to administration's concerns. I feel that it is primarily my responsibility as chair to be a boundary spanner and get this information for the department. I will be meeting again with the dean in the next two weeks on these matters. Once I get a clear understanding of administration expectations, then we as a faculty will need to consider the desires and If and how we can meet them.

- We need to rethink our advising. Our block advising consistently results in complaints to the dean's office. I understand our department has more complaints than any other department. There are two major types of complaints: 1) our advisors have a bad attitude (they do not want to do this), and 2) the advisors are poorly trained (they do not know the technical regulations, do not attend training sessions, do not call the dean's office with questions, and give bad advice). Any suggestions are welcome at this point.

Figure 3.2 Memorandum cont.

---

3. GREATER VISIBILITY FOR THE DEPARTMENT

We need to have a higher profile as a department for our research, teaching, and service activities. Here are some ideas about how we can do this:

- As I indicated in my earlier memo, this department has an excellent teaching and research record. We need recognition for this. I would like each of you to summarize one of your recent publications, research streams, or research activities into layperson's terms and either directly contact the media or give me that summary. Also highlight your noteworthy teaching accomplishments and service contributions. We will be preparing a media release for the recent focus groups and hope to use these to get into several media outlets.

- We need to serve on more high visibility university committees. If any of you are interested, please let me know. My Committee Manual lists 65 possible choices. Select your committees carefully; some would be killers for untenured faculty. Consult me or other senior faculty before you agree to participate.

4. EXTERNAL FUNDING

We need to become resource independent from the dean. To this aim:

- We need to develop and cultivate ties with potential donors. I would like faculty to try to develop grants and get monies that support our mission. As chair, I will take a lead role in getting funds and am closely working with the development office now on several projects. Please bring your ideas in this area to our next faculty meeting.

In sum, I see great potential for departmental growth and these are only a few ideas that can take us into a favored departmental position. Please react to these ideas (directly to me if you will not be at the next faculty meeting). I am very open to new ideas.

---

process), a statement of the department's priorities can be a most effective vehicle for fulfilling one of your roles as chair: to inspire.

From key outcomes to department goals

With vision/mission developed and with key outcome areas identified and described, you are ready to discuss your department's goals. Department goals give direction and encourage action. Most goal-oriented studies give evidence that performance is enhanced in the pursuit of specific targets. While many administrators agree with these studies, few seem to regularly use any type of formal goal-setting process in their own organizations. Many reasons are given for this; the following come from practicing department chairs:

- Previous experiences with goal setting that were difficult to administer or unclear in their results
- Personal belief that goal setting adds extra paperwork to an already heavy administrative workload
- Lack of knowledge concerning the goal-setting process or the inability to develop quality goals related to department priorities
- Difficulties discussing department goals with faculty and tying individual faculty goals to department goals.

If you've shied away from goal setting for reasons such as these, you should rethink your position. An active planning process can impact department unity and enhance department achievement (Amit, Lucier, Hitt, and Nixon 2002; Buller 2006; Burke 2005; Foskett and Lumby 2003; Shulman 2007).

An overwhelming number of studies provide specific support for the goal setting process. One review of such studies offers impressive evidence that goal setting improves performance (Latham and Yukl 1975). Another, independent analysis of over one hundred well designed field- and lab-studies from 1969 to 1980 further supports the positive relationship between goal setting and performance (Latham and Steele 1983). These and other reports form a combined list of over two hundred separate studies that testify to the strong relationship between goal setting and productivity (Katzell and Guzzo 1983).

The basic premise of goal-setting theory seems obvious: "the conscious intentions of people influence their actions and behavior." The real questions, of course, are "What actions?" and "To what end?" The conclusions drawn from the many goal-setting studies mentioned above are not consistent in all dimensions, but several common principles emerge from them. Setting goals tends to improve organizational performance *to the degree that*:

1. The goals are specific, measurable, and clearly stated.

2. The goals are set at high levels of achievement, but still remain within reasonable realms of attainment.

3. Regular attention and feedback is provided.

4. Each goal is related to key organizational outcomes.

Setting your department's goals

Establishing vision/mission and identifying key outcome areas are meant, primarily, to encourage unity and inspire excellence in the long term. Setting goals, on the other hand, shifts the focus to short-term (usually a one-year horizon) effort and activity. By tying each department goal to one or more key outcome areas, you can define measurable achievements of highest value to your department and college. Department goals lay out, in writing, the accomplishments that are important this year to you, to your faculty, and to your dean. Thus, department goals must be clear, challenging, and achievable during the next planning time period.

As discussed earlier, be sure to review your department's goals to see if they:

- are specifically explained (and can be measured)
- are challenging (and are realistically achievable)
- can be used to provide feedback to faculty members and to administrators

- are directly related to one or more of your department's broad priorities.

Examples of department goals related to each of our previously suggested key outcome areas are shown in Table 3.4. These examples show the level of specificity and measurability needed to make goals effective.

Building a strong relationship between department goals (short term) and key outcome areas (long term) can provide an emotional unity and sense of direction to your department. To make yourself more familiar with this process, review the key outcome areas of your department's vision/mission by using Exercise 3.4, and consider one or two measurable goals for each area.

Other measurable goals are suggested here to give you some ideas with which to build your own set of department goals. Look at them as starting points for brainstorming and discussion, not as recommendations to be used for your unique department.

- *Student learning:* standardized score levels, student evaluations, admission ratios, placement data, program completion ratios, individual knowledge and skill-development levels, alumni accomplishments, diversity of student body

- *Faculty achievement:* department publication record, faculty evaluation levels, department record of grants and grant proposals, student/faculty ratios, national recognition in discipline, relevance of academic programs, faculty/student relations, department teaching quality

- *Constituent relations:* coordination with other departments, activity with other colleges, relationships with government agencies, involvement with employer groups, membership in professional associations

- *Academic process:* department goal-setting process, program evaluation systems, chair evaluations, levels of faculty involvement, department resource allocation and budget priorities, faculty collegiality, department diversity

- *Department resources:* resource utilization, department results and outcome measures, college and university resources allocations, grants, partnerships, private funding

Department success is not accomplished simply by providing written statements of direction and intent. Frequently and consistently sharing your vision with your staff and faculty is the critical issue. Your role as department chair is to lead the faculty in effecting the changes that will get results. Motivating individuals to act toward the realization of the department's goals is the primary challenge of your leadership position. This challenge is addressed in chapter 4.

Table 3.4 Sample Goals Related to each Key Outcome Area

STUDENT LEARNING

1. Increase the ratio of students completing their degree programs to at least 80% by the end of the year.

2. Develop a department system to track all graduates and record their placement and work data for a five-year period following graduation.

3. Organize a faculty task team to analyze, revise, and update the department measures of student achievement.

FACULTY ACHIEVEMENT

4. Increase the number of top-tier faculty publications in the department by 15% each year for the next five years.

5. Appoint a faculty task team to review all undergraduate curricula with a recommendation by year's end to streamline current offerings on the basis of relevance, student demand, and employer interests.

6. Improve the department's overall teaching-effectiveness rating to an average of 3.00 (on a 4.00 scale) and reduce the number of ratings below minimum (2.00) to less than 10% of all teacher ratings.

CONSTITUENT RELATIONS

7. Develop an advocate relationship with the director (or key staff) of the Federal Science Foundation. (This is not a goal of the chair, but of the department as a whole.)

8. Initiate an employer advisory board (or increase the number of members on the current advisory board).

9. Improve department visibility to field constituents by raising the number of field contacts by at least twenty-five next year. These will be coordinated through the department secretary.

ACADEMIC PROCESS

10. Initiate a formal faculty planning system within the department to be ready for implementation at the beginning of the next academic year.

11. Work with the dean and staff to develop a better database of budget information for monitoring, evaluating, and projecting department budgets.

12. Automate all student records within the next three years. Develop a new system that would allow PhD records to be automated by the end of this year, all graduate records by the second year, and to include all student records by year three.

DEPARTMENT RESOURCES

13. Increase the amount of planned-giving from department constituents by 50% of last year's totals.

14. Hire a new staff member before the end of summer to provide grant-preparation support to faculty.

Exercise 3.4 Department Goals Worksheet

Your vision/mission, including key outcome areas, sets your long-term orientation to the department's future. Following from this orientation, your department's goals provide focus for planning the activities and achievements that will be important in the coming year. Before preparing your department's goals, review your environmental analyses and examine each of your key outcome areas from Exercise 3.3. Then, for each key outcome, prepare a written goal of measurable achievement for the year. These goals may not deliver the final, long-term success hoped for in each area, but will initiate effort in the right direction.

KEY OUTCOME I: STUDENT LEARNING

Measurable goal statement #1

Measurable goal statement #2

Measurable goal statement #3

KEY OUTCOME II: FACULTY ACHIEVEMENT

Measurable goal statement #1

Measurable goal statement #2

Measurable goal statement #3

KEY OUTCOME III: CONSTITUENT RELATIONS

Measurable goal statement #1

Measurable goal statement #2

Measurable goal statement #3

KEY OUTCOME IV: OTHER

Measurable goal statement #1

Measurable goal statement #2

## Chapter 4

DEPARTMENT RESULTS

Goal Setting and Action Planning

> I find the great thing in this world is not where we stand,
> but in what direction we are moving.
> — Oliver Wendell Holmes

You've analyzed your department, identified your mission and key outcome areas, and developed this year's goals. As your initial department-planning meeting comes to a close, you hand out your written plan and deliver an impassioned plea for faculty support and involvement. Your faculty members respond with enthusiasm, excitedly place the new planning document in their briefcases—and complacently head back to their separate offices and individual interests.

The call for leadership discussed in chapter 1 is not a rhetorical imperative. Integrating your department plan into the lives of faculty and staff requires communication and action. This is what breathes life into the department leadership model. To personalize this challenge, ask yourself two questions:

1. With you as chair, will your department achieve more than it would have otherwise?

2. How do you plan to have this effect on your department's future?

Lieberson and O'Connor (1972) proposed that an organization's success may be impacted more by its external environments than its managers. This may not be surprising, since organizational success is defined as the organization's responsiveness to its environmental conditions, especially as those conditions change. But effective chairs do more than react and adapt to their environments. More recent studies support leadership as the primary force in an organization's performance. This is particularly true when leaders (proactive) are distinguished from managers (reactive) (House and Baetz 1979; Rosser, Johnsrud, and Heck 2003; Rost 1995; Smith, Carson, and Alexander 1984; Thomas and Bainbridge 2002; Weiner and Mahoney 1981). When it comes to your department's future, your skills will make a difference.

The department leadership model (Figure 4.1) places this implementation process in perspective as it addresses the question, "How will you influence department productivity?" Effective implementation engages your staff and faculty, and is the key to your effectiveness as department chair.

DEPARTMENT RESULTS:
HOW WILL YOU INFLUENCE PRODUCTIVITY?

As you anticipate your involvement with individual staff and faculty, don't forget the challenge discussed in chapter 2: developing an academic team. Your department's team attitude begins with you. As you interact with your faculty, always keep your attention on:

- encouraging their activities and decisions in accordance with the department's mission/goals,
- supporting individual-performance goals and personal achievements, and
- creating enjoyable relationships.

Effective team climate not only adds value, but also makes for a better place to work. You don't need everyone to agree with everything all of the time, but mutual respect and good humor are imperative. Life is simply too short to suffer the alternatives.

For department chairs, influencing individuals employs two dimensions of leadership skill: encouraging your support staff and convincing your faculty. Most faculty members are interested in "rational explanations of purposes" and "support from administration and colleagues." On the other hand, department staff will be most influenced with a show of "confidence and support through effective delegation" (Keys and Case 1990, 42).

These differences derive at least in part from the professional stature of faculty. Since faculty members are colleagues as well as experts in their respective disciplines, they typically expect to be more involved in departmental goal setting and decision making. In contrast, your support staff will be more directly responsible for department programs and activities. The appropriate leadership style will not be the same for your staff as for your faculty. Don't expect it to be either simple or easy, but you will need to decide, 1) how much to involve each person in "setting" department goals and, 2) how to encourage "participation" when implementing those goals. Recall that setting goals for the department (see chapter 3) requires a strong connection to an identified vision/mission. Set-

Figure 4.1 Department leadership Model: Department Results

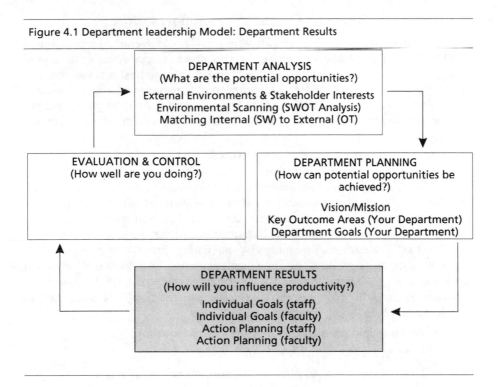

ting individual goals provides the details for moving toward that vision/mission. Understanding this relationship is a critical first step in building a team attitude.

Faculty involvement is frequently different from staff involvement. The members of each group will have different skills, abilities, and needs, and you will find different reasons at different times for inviting their participation in the goal-setting process. At this stage, faculty involvement generally takes precedence. Imagine, by way of illustration, that your department has decided to reduce the number of majors offered, or create a new major in a growing field. Staff participation in this decision may not be necessary, as it requires specific discipline expertise, but faculty involvement will be critical.

As you involve faculty and staff, your challenge is to determine their appropriate levels of participation in setting their goals. Individual goals must contribute to department success, but because faculty members are experts in their disciplines, you cannot simply dictate what their goals will be. There are two stages to individual goal setting: first, the setting of an individual's goals in support of department goals (individual goal setting); second, the actions taken by the individual to accomplish those goals (individual action planning). Leaving the discussion of individual action planning to the next section of this chapter, let us turn our attention to individual goal setting at your staff and faculty levels.

Individual goals: Your support staff

As discussed in chapter 3, department goals guide overall direction, but it is difficult for staff members to derive their individual responsibilities from general guidelines. Setting individual staff goals is one of your best ways to communicate specific direction. Every individual needs to know the department's goals, but every individual also needs to know how he or she, as an individual, will be involved in achieving those goals. This is what gives impetus to people's activity.

How many staff members report to you at this time? What are their job duties? Have you sufficiently communicated to them the department's mission, key outcome areas, and annual goals? Do they understand their specific responsibilities in achieving those goals? Your staff's involvement, effort, and contribution are essential to moving the department in the direction you've envisioned. Support staff are there to serve the department's needs, and, as noted earlier, you can best influence staff members by delegating their specific responsibilities and generously recognizing their achievements. You must set individual goals for them, goals that direct their particular activities toward the broader department mission. In relation to each of the department's key outcome areas, individual staff goals should focus on:

- activities and programs to support student learning,
- support for faculty achievement,
- internal systems to improve academic achievement, and
- support systems to build constituent relationships.

Not all staff members will need a specific goal for each department goal, but you must see to it that individual goals are set when needed. Review your department's goals and determine which of them will require staff assistance. Whether your staff members develop their own goals with your input or you set them after staff discussions, it is important to state them clearly and in writing. It is always wise to solicit input from your staff during this process. However, it may be counter-productive to encourage the staff's full participation in setting their goals when the department's systems are already determined or when you have already established goals for the department as a whole. Staff members' autonomy, involvement, and personal growth will come more from allowing them to decide *how* to best accomplish their goals than from rehashing goals that, in reality, are set. The difference between goal *setting* (what is to be done) and goal *implementing* (how it is to be done) is critical to your staff; cognizance of this distinction can improve staff productivity and will be discussed further in the next section of this chapter.

Of course, individual staff goals must be prepared with actual target measures (percentages, amounts, numbers, deadlines, etc.) and must clearly specify any support systems or resources needed. Examples of individual objectives compatible with the department's goals are shown in Table 4.1.

Table 4.1 Staff Accountabilities: Examples for Consideration

DEPARTMENT GOALS	STAFF FOCUS	EXAMPLES FOR CONSIDERATION
Student Outcomes	Activities and Programs	• improved record systems
		• innovative alumni-tracking
		• surveys and analyses
		• informational reports
		• student diversity identification
		• lab support
		• advising programs
Faculty Achievement	Faculty Support	• clerical support
		• word-processing support
		• research support
		• grant proposal support
		• feedback systems
		• instructional support
Academic Process	Internal Systems	• computer assistance
		• technical training
		• program evaluation
		• budget information
		• internal communication
		• facilities maintenance
Constituent Relations	Constituent Support Systems	• media coverage
		• advisory-board planning
		• networking information
		• development programs
		• stakeholder analysis
		• public relations and clientele
		• rapport

Review your department goals from the exercise in chapter 3 and identify which staff members should be directly involved in each key area. Then propose individual goals by which selected staff members can contribute to department goals. Staff input and discussion are useful here, but keep in mind that the purpose of this process is to assign individual staff accountability (delegation) for measurable results. Make these assignments clearly, and then encourage your staff to use their own initiative to decide *how* to carry the assignments out. As you prepare these individual goal statements, focus on the degree to which they: 1) are specific, measurable, and clearly stated; 2) are set at high levels of achievement, but remain within the reasonable realms of individual capabilities; 3) are directly related to department goals; and 4) establish accountability for and provide feedback to the individual.

Individual goals: Your academic faculty

As you review your department's goals, ask yourself who will accomplish them—they cannot be realized alone. Your staff will assist you as discussed, but only so far as their efforts are appropriately directed (delegated). Achieving department goals requires the expertise and knowledge of your faculty. Your leadership challenge is to actively involve your faculty in the implementation process by having them set their individual goals (Buller 2006; Coleman 2004; Morrill 2007).

Involving faculty is a delicate process. While the department's mission and success are certainly desirable for everyone, chairs must remind themselves that individual faculty goals always take first priority. That is the way it should be. Universities and academic departments widely report three basic categories of faculty outcomes: teaching, research, and service. These categories remain a viable guide for encouraging specific goals for each faculty member. You'll notice that all three are closely related to your department's key outcome areas; this connection is the key to influencing your faculty. Your efforts must not be directed toward establishing equal goals for each faculty member, but toward *balancing* individual faculty goals with overall department goals. As with any organizational effort, the key to success lies in making individual faculty goals compatible with the goals of the department.

While department goals may (by necessity) be determined by the chair, individual faculty goals must be developed and determined by the faculty members themselves. Thus, the role of department chair is not to develop annual goals for faculty members, but to share a vision of the future and encourage, excite, or inspire them to develop individual goals that support these departmental directions. Regular discussion with each faculty member is both desirable and necessary. Your role is to encourage your faculty to develop individual goals that will:

1. demonstrate excellence and garner recognition in their academic disciplines,

2. encourage individual growth and development,

3. identify challenging results (measurable) to be achieved during the coming year, and

4. connect their successes to the key outcome areas of the department.

Remember, individual faculty goals must also meet the criteria of measurability, challenge, and attainability. Most importantly, this process provides a vehicle for you to discuss the faculty's individual efforts and achievements. What better way to encourage discussion and activity than to focus on the self-initiated goals of your faculty members? As you discuss these, try to express two or three key outcome areas from your mission/vision statement in terms of faculty outcome categories (teaching, research, and service). Below is list of sample measures to consider:

TEACHING

- student evaluations
- student learning
- course load
- class size
- class projects and independent studies
- class innovations and new course development

RESEARCH

- number and level of publications
- number and type of papers presented
- number of grant proposals
- grant acceptances
- ongoing streams of research
- research activity with other faculty members and other universities

SERVICE

- student advising/counseling
- college- or university-committee assignments
- department programs or assignments
- professional memberships or positions
- outreach to external constituencies
- approved consulting activity
- personal development activity

Exercise 4.1 is an example of one department's faculty planning guide. Use this, revise it, or create your own using the appropriate measurable parameters. (If you are developing this form for your own individual goals, add at least one additional category of professional development that specifies growth in each of the department chair roles discussed in chapter 1: manager, leader, faculty developer, and scholar.)

As discussed earlier, the professional status of faculty members makes their participation essential during the development of faculty goals. Thus, the faculty planning guide is an excellent tool for influencing the faculty's focus and effort without overriding individual voices. Encourage your faculty members to develop challenging goals—based on their own strengths—that will help them succeed as individuals and will contribute to the department's overall success.

ACTION PLANNING
TO ENCOURAGE INDIVIDUAL ACTIVITY

To this point, our discussion has focused on developing individual goals that will support department goals. We now turn to the other half of the delegation question: getting it done.

Clearly, goal-achievement will not just happen. It requires decisive action and individual effort. Many sources have defined "action-planning" as the process by which such effort and activity is initiated (Drucker 1974; Thompson, Strickland, and Gamble 2005; Steiner 1979; Yavitz and Newman 1982). In simple terms, action plans state the specific, sequential activities needed to accomplish a given goal or objective. They further identify the individual responsible for each activity and the specific time frame within which each step will be completed. Action-planning forms (as shown in Figure 4.2) are available in most formal management programs; they are common and usually self-explanatory.

Quite often, especially in professional organizations, action planning is misunderstood and misused. When action plans are required by the system, they tend to create additional, non-productive work and to precipitate directive leadership by default. Action planning needs to be available, but self-selected. Depending on individuals' roles in the department, self-selection will take different forms. It is therefore useful to recall, in broad terms, the different ways in which the chair, the faculty, and the staff relate to the department's goals:

- Chairs provide long-term department direction (mission, key outcomes, and goals).
- Faculty contribute academic expertise to goal setting and initiate action planning.
- Staff report more directly to the chair as they contribute to the action planning process.

Exercise 4.1 Faculty Planning Guide

DEPARTMENT OF:

NAME OF FACULTY MEMBER:

I. TEACHING

A. FORMAL INSTRUCTION

Course	Number of students	Student ratings

New courses to be developed

B. INFORMAL INSTRUCTION

1. Student Advising:

# of undergraduate advisees:	
# of master's advisees:	
# of doctoral advisees:	

2. Project, Thesis, Dissertation (If Applicable).

# students with independent study projects	
# master's students at thesis stage	
# doctoral students at dissertation stage	
List your students who will be completing thesis or dissertation this year	

3. Other:

II. RESEARCH/SCHOLARLY ACTIVITY

A. FOCUS OF SCHOLARSHIP (RESEARCH STREAM):

Exercise 4.1 Faculty Planning Guide cont

B. MANUSCRIPTS (BOOKS, MONOGRAPHS, ARTICLES, AND PAPERS, PLANNED OR IN PROCESS):

Planned	Intended Audience	Title or Journal	Completion Date

C. GRANTS, GRANT PROPOSALS, OR OTHER DEVELOPMENT PROJECTS:

Title	Planned	Submitted	Accepted

D. PRESENTATIONS

	Title	Subject/place/audience	Planned Date
1. Original or keynote			
2. Secondary			

III. SERVICE

A. DEPARTMENT / COLLEGE:

B. UNIVERSITY:

C. COMMUNITY/STATE/REGIONAL CONSTITUENCIES:

D. NATIONAL/INTERNATIONAL

IV. PROFESSIONAL DEVELOPMENT PLANS

70

Action planning, when implemented properly, serves both individuals within the department and the department as a whole. Its benefits fit into five interrelated categories:

1. *Initiative and impetus.* Action planning helps individuals find a starting point for progress toward demanding goals.

    A staff member assigned the goal of expanding the department's available lab space may have a good general idea of what is required, but not be too sure of what comes first—room, equipment, a demand study, funding sources, or faculty agreement. Preparing an action plan (Figure 4.2) not only identifies the first step, but can have a galvanizing effect by specifying who will take this first step, and how.

2. *Approach, activities, and sequence.* Action planning determines the specific steps, proper sequence, and appropriate time frame for activities needed to accomplish a given goal.

    Newer faculty members determined to upgrade the quality of their research publications can use an action plan to identify journal options, co-authorship potentials, and colleague review panels. They can also create a concrete writing schedule.

3. *Coordination of resources.* Action planning provides a vehicle for coordinating effort, accessing resources, and enlisting other individuals in the achievement of selected goals.

    Chairs faced with the difficult and complex goal of revising the department's curriculum may greatly benefit from an action plan detailing the steps, time frames, and accountabilities required. The inclusion of staff, faculty, or other administrators can be facilitated by knowing not only who is needed, but what they can do and when they can do it.

4. *Innovation and suggestion.* Action planning provides a framework for soliciting ideas on how to undertake unfamiliar tasks or approach difficult goals.

    Faculty challenged to improve their teaching might not be open, normally, to critique or suggestions from others, but be willing to seek such assistance in the process of developing action plans at their own initiative. Action plans for individuals can accomplish great things when encouraged judiciously, but can be self-defeating if they are officially required and reviewed by the system. The value of action plans lies in the process of developing them, not in their evaluation.

Figure 4.2 Action Planning Form

INDIVIDUAL GOAL STATEMENT:		

ACTION PLAN TO ACCOMPLISH ABOVE GOAL:		
Specific Action Steps	Planned Completion Date	Person Accountable for this Step
1.		
2.		
3.		
4.		
5.		
6.		
7.		
8.		

5. *Progress and communication.* Action-planning allows individuals to communicate progress toward goals that otherwise may be difficult to evaluate.

A staff goal to automate student records may need some method of interim reporting. If the new record system will not be operational until its completion, action plans will be useful in identifying signposts of progress.

Notice that the benefits listed above are more for the individual than the department. Action planning is for individuals. Benefits to the department are real, but must remain secondary. Action plans will not be needed for all department goals or for all individuals. However, they are valuable to the staff member, faculty member, or department chair who is faced with a particularly difficult, new, or complex goal. Your challenge is to decide when action plans will assist, rather than hinder, individual performance.

Faculty action planning

Faculty goals are best developed by faculty. Action planning for faculty can be suggested and encouraged by department chairs, but should be developed or reviewed by the chair only at the invitation of the faculty member. Your influence, when used wisely, can be significant in this process, but deciding how to accomplish individual goals is best left to each faculty member. Suggest action planning to faculty members when they want to move in a new direction, or need help realizing difficult aspirations. If no particular difficulties are indicated, there is little need to review their implementation plans. This part of the planning process is for their use and benefit. You can assist, support, and suggest faculty action planning, but to be effective, the plans should remain a faculty prerogative.

Staff action planning

Staff performance requires more direct input, as your staff initiates activity toward department goals. But even here, you should provide direction with a light hand, basing your involvement on each staff member's skills, experience, and initiative. As you review staff progress toward individual goals, request action plans only for those goals not being accomplished. Action plans for routine or easily achievable goals do not typically improve performance. Even when it comes to complex goals, have your staff develop their own action plans, offering input and assistance only as needed. Action plans developed by your staff can be reviewed, but typically are not to be collected and evaluated. *The action plan is less for the department than for the individual.* With the understanding that you are managing individuals, assess the value of recommending action plans and determine how prepared your staff members are to create their own.

You will be better prepared to mentor your support staff if you have used action planning yourself. As an exercise, use the action-plan form (Figure 4.2) to identify a department goal that might be difficult to accomplish or that is particularly important to your dean, and practice developing an action plan for yourself.

Take these steps as you prepare your action plan:

1. List all major activities (action steps) that you anticipate being important to the objective. This will organize the process in your mind and prevent the appearance of inactivity. It really does help with setting the process in motion.

2. Indicate the planned or *expected completion dates* for the action steps. This will coordinate effort and encourage action within acceptable time frames.

3. Specify *who will be accountable* for the completion of each action step. Notice that some of the steps in your action plan may very well become individual goals for your staff. Also note whether coordination is needed with faculty, the dean's office, other departments, or external constituents; this action plan presents an excellent vehicle for communicating your support needs.

Remember, action plans should be developed by the individual. You're creating *your* action plan for *your* goal. This exercise will help you explain to staff or faculty how they can prepare their own action plans, but it does not imply that you should develop action plans for anyone but yourself. Action planning should not be perceived as a burden, or as an unwelcome additional assignment. Action plans are meant solely to support activity toward individual goal accomplishment.

Evaluation and Control: How Well Are You Doing?

Since this chapter is titled "Department Results," it seems reasonable to conclude with a discussion of evaluation and control systems. The term "control" frequently has a negative connotation in the academic environment. However, within an academic department, control should not mean monitoring or checking up on the daily activities of staff or faculty. The value and purpose of control should lie in helping individuals become more successful in accomplishing their personal goals as they contribute to the department's vision/mission. Specifically, the evaluation and control process should:

- *recognize* individual excellence and achievement,
- *encourage* individual productivity (specifically in relation to key outcome areas), and
- *suggest and assist* the development of individual action plans in areas identified needing emphasis or improvement.

Figure 4.3 presents the full department leadership model, in which the evaluation and control component forms a link between department results (individual achievements) and department plans (vision/mission/goals).

Control is best exercised in the context of plans made and results achieved. Without plans or achievements, there is nothing to evaluate. The question of "Where do you want to be?" must precede the question of "How well are you doing?" When goal setting and action planning ("How do you plan

Figure 4.3 Department Leadership Model: Evaluation and Control

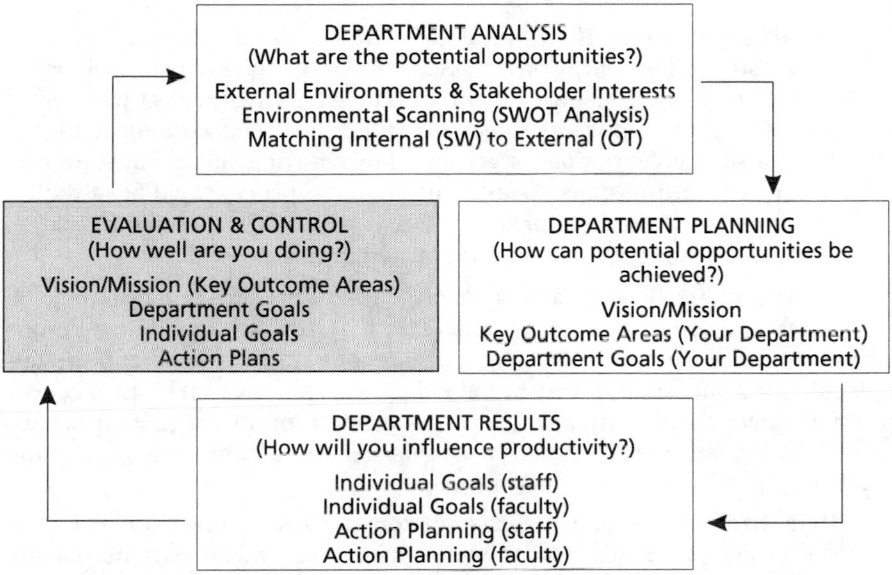

```
┌─────────────────────────────────────────────┐
│              DEPARTMENT ANALYSIS              │
│       (What are the potential opportunities?) │
│                                               │
│   External Environments & Stakeholder Interests│
│      Environmental Scanning (SWOT Analysis)   │
│        Matching Internal (SW) to External (OT)│
└─────────────────────────────────────────────┘

┌──────────────────────────┐  ┌──────────────────────────────┐
│   EVALUATION & CONTROL    │  │      DEPARTMENT PLANNING       │
│   (How well are you doing?)│  │ (How can potential opportunities be │
│                           │  │          achieved?)            │
│ Vision/Mission (Key Outcome Areas)│  │                          │
│     Department Goals      │  │         Vision/Mission         │
│      Individual Goals     │  │ Key Outcome Areas (Your Department)│
│        Action Plans       │  │ Department Goals (Your Department)│
└──────────────────────────┘  └──────────────────────────────┘

┌─────────────────────────────────────────────┐
│              DEPARTMENT RESULTS               │
│      (How will you influence productivity?)   │
│                                               │
│          Individual Goals (staff)             │
│          Individual Goals (faculty)           │
│           Action Planning (staff)             │
│           Action Planning (faculty)           │
└─────────────────────────────────────────────┘
```

to get there?") are included, they provide a vehicle not only for monitoring status, but also for encouraging progress.

The control process is not about recording activities or evaluating performance: it's about recognizing and encouraging plans and achievements. It will include annual reviews, but require frequent informal discussions to be meaningful. As you encourage your staff and faculty to greater productivity, meet with them informally and often. An effective control process will have the following three priorities:

1. *Long-term department success.* Consistently and continuously focus on the department's mission and key outcome areas. This is the "single mindedness" so important to effective leaders. Whether with your staff or faculty, your first priority is to communicate what the department needs. These discussions need not be lengthy or heavily detailed, but are valuable for two reasons: first, they set the direction or basis for developing individual goals; second, they encourage meaningful feedback concerning those goals.

2. *Individual goal achievement.* For each key outcome area, your role is to influence and support individual achievement. Discussing individual goals is one of your best opportunities for building the department's success. As you encourage progress toward individual goals, examine the value and relevance of these goals to the department. Your aim is to get staff and faculty excited about accom-

plishing individual goals that are personally rewarding and contribute to department priorities.

3. *Action planning.* If individual goals are not being achieved, the final step in the control process is to encourage and evaluate specific activity toward achieving them. Don't fall into the "activity trap" of valuing action plans as ends unto themselves. Encouraging action plans is a great option for getting things moving and building productive relationships. Assessment of action plans should be at the invitation of your staff or faculty, and can be used as an interim measure of progress toward individual achievement.

Understanding the contrasts between goal setting and action planning will allow you to discuss, coach, and initiate activity toward department results *through* individual achievements. Your discussions are likely to differ from staff to faculty, and will certainly vary by individual. This process can be an excellent tool for influencing faculty members. The question of how well your department is doing becomes a productive discussion when complemented by the rewards of individual accomplishments.

Refer back to your department's mission and key outcome areas, and revisit the goals you've planned. As you influence individual staff and faculty achievements, keep a close eye on their contributions to department success. This final control process may simply entail deciding which goals for faculty and which action plans for staff merit your attention. Use your judgment, your imagination, and your leadership skills, always being sure to listen carefully.

Your challenge as department chair is to cultivate a team attitude that encourages individual excellence, strengthens relationships among faculty and staff, and celebrates long-term department success. Inspire your staff and faculty members to develop and accomplish individual goals that, when combined with those of all others in the department, will contribute to collective priorities and successes. Don't reduce your control activities to additional steps in the sequence of department management. Integrate those functions into your leadership plans for the future. Remember, these are your responsibilities, your decisions, and your future; consider them carefully, attend to them consciously, and enjoy the process.

Chapter 5

MANAGING TIME

For Department Chairs Only

> Time is the coin of your life. It is the only coin you have,
> and only you can determine how it will be spent.
> Be careful lest you let other people spend it for you.
> — Carl Sandburg

"I didn't have enough time to get it all done." "There just aren't enough hours in the day anymore." "The week is almost over and I haven't yet found the time to start my top priority project." "If I want this job done right, I'll have to do it myself." "I guess this project will have to be mine, because it's just too important to assign to a faculty member." "I'll assign this project to a staff member just as soon as I get it off and running."

Need more hours in the day? Yes, but getting more hours is not a possibility. Every person gets exactly the same number of hours each day. Rather than attempting to expand the time, it is more productive to examine the problems that are within your control: fear of offending, wanting to do projects yourself, reluctance to delegate, not setting priorities, the desire to avoid conflict, and so on.

Moving from the autonomy, scholarship, independence, and individualism of a faculty member to the accountability, administravia, social interaction, and accessibility of a department chair are the important transitions of moving from faculty to chair, as discussed in chapter 1. These transitions typically entail the addition, not the substitution, of responsibilities; newly appointed chairs are often faced with the need to continue their professional achievements while significantly increasing their administrative workload—all with the same amount of time available.

Time has always been a concern of department chairs. But trying to find more time is neither prudent nor productive. The cliché holds true: "It's not how much time you have that matters, but what you do with the time you have." Time becomes problematic for department chairs as, 1) their stress levels increase with added responsibilities, and 2) they see a decrease in the time available for their personal and professional interests. In a survey of over one thousand department chairs, the top five items reported as contributing most to the chairs' stress levels were:

1. inability to keep current in the discipline or find time to publish,

2. insufficient budget,

3. evaluation of and interaction with faculty members,

4. work-related activities conflicting with personal activities,

5. unrealistic self-expectations. (Gmelch et al. 1992)

All five of these top stressors relate to the chair's time problems. The struggle to keep current in the field by maintaining quality research-streams will create stress for research-oriented chairs. Budget difficulties and faculty interactions are time-consuming and can be stressful for all department chairs. The responsibilities that come with the chair's position will siphon time from professional and personal activities. And it is frequently chairs' unrealistic expectation that they will be able to meet their responsibilities without re-evaluating their time commitments that adds a significant level of stress to their daily lives.

TIME: THE PROBLEM

In another survey, over one hundred department chairs indicated that they spent the majority of their time preparing reports and budgets, scheduling activities, and interacting with faculty (Meredith and Wunsch 1991). They spent the least time doing scholarly research and professional study in their academic disciplines. Reduced availability of time for personal and professional growth continues to be the problem for most department chairs.

In many time-management seminars, the emphasis is on identifying "time wasters" and managing priorities to reduce or avoid them. There is much agreement that budgets, reports, correspondence, and various other types of paperwork are a major consumer of chairs' time. Unplanned interruptions (e.g., visitors and phone calls) and too many unnecessary meetings are also widely reported as major time wasters. While it is always good to reduce or avoid such drains on your time, this is seldom sufficient to solve the entire problem. As department chair, your main priority isn't finding more time, taking on fewer tasks, or culling the tasks that are wasteful; your main priority is gaining more control over your activities and, thus, the way your time is distributed.

TIME: THE ISSUE

I. Terry Adams, the newly appointed chair in a department of anthropology, has just spent the entire afternoon trying to resolve a serious scheduling problem brought to light by the department secretary.

II. Terry spent the majority of last week preparing an unplanned budget report and resolving an unexpected disagreement between two faculty members.

III. Two weeks ago, Terry was approached by a government agency requesting on-site visits with the entire faculty. Thus, this week has been spent in a series of meetings with the faculty and several university administrators.

IV. Yesterday, Terry was called in for an unscheduled work session with the dean to discuss the status of the curriculum-revision project.

In each of these instances, the problem is not what the new department chair is doing, but who is in control. In all four cases, someone else is determining what to do and when to do it.

Of course, in none of the above cases can the chair refuse to cooperate; nor can he or she resolve the problems without devoting time to them. But their own time-management considerations demand that chairs acquire some control over both the content (what) and the timing (when) of their activities. Paradoxically, managing your time tends to conflict with managing your department. As chair, you need to maintain good working relations with your dean, your faculty and colleagues (internal and external), and your staff, even though it is they who create the bulk of your time-management difficulties. All three groups are vying for control.

While each of these is in some part outside of your direct influence, it becomes your challenge as department chair to increase the amount of self-controlled time at your disposal. In Case I above, it was a staff member who dictated the what and when of Terry Adams's time. In Cases II and III, it was colleagues (i.e., faculty members and external constituents). In Case IV, it was the dean (i.e., the boss). Time management requires you to think not only about what you do with your time, but also about who determines what you do and when you do it.

Department chairs may allow others to exercise control over their activities for various reasons. Chief among these reasons is the (often unconscious) unwillingness to make unpopular or difficult choices. At times, avoiding a decision may seem like the best way to maintain an important relationship. Yet in most situations, such avoidance simply delays the strain in the relationship while eroding your control over your job. For example, if only one additional faculty position has been funded for the coming year and you have two faculty groups vying for that position, postponing your decision is not likely to strengthen faculty relationships and is quite likely to increase the interruptions you suffer from both faculty groups. On the other hand, a reasoned decision shared with both faculty groups, while surely the more difficult choice, is certain to afford you more control over how you will resolve the problem.

The *problem* of time is stress, which is caused by non-productive activity and the limitations placed on your personal and professional development. The *issue* of time management is control: How can you prevent others from controlling the timing and content of your job? How can you sustain the control needed to spend your time productively? Your control as department chair emerges as you set clear priorities and make definitive, though often difficult, choices in relation to those priorities.

Time: The Solution

Effective time management involves the following four areas, which will have the most direct influence on your decisions:

1. Unexpected or unplanned interruptions from students, staff, colleagues, administrators, or other stakeholders

2. Formal meetings, planned or unplanned, with any of the above constituents

3. Discussions, evaluations, and other interactions with faculty and staff

4. Personal decisions.

Unplanned interruptions

There is much written, discussed, and understood about the problems of unscheduled visits and phone calls, but how can chairs gain more control over these interruptions without sacrificing strong working relationships? While delegation is often cited as the key to many of your time-management problems, two concepts seem more relevant to this particular issue: First is the recognition of your management team, or "management molecule." Rather than seeing yourself as managing downward to your staff and faculty, imagine that you are the center of a management molecule: the dean is above, your support staff is below, faculty members and other administrators are to one side, and your external constituents are to the other (Figure 5.1). This adds new dimensionality

Figure 5.1 Your Management Team

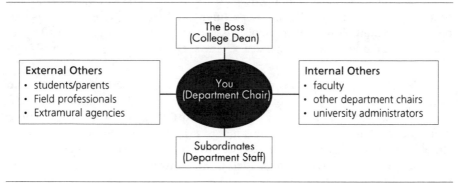

to your management. Perhaps people with less relevance (those not attached to your management molecule) should not be given significant time in your busy schedule.

Second is the specific assignment of responsibility for the next action step, often paired with the "monkey on your back" metaphor (Oncken and Wass 1974). Instead of flailing at a monkey on your back, you might consider who has the next move—i.e., on whose back should the monkey be placed? Too often, our greatest time problem lies with our decision as to who should take the next action, rather than whether the responsibility should be fully delegated.

In Case I, Terry Adams chose to get involved immediately in solving the scheduling problem. This resulted in a solution, but at the expense of time and effort that Terry had planned to use elsewhere. A more profitable first reaction would have been to determine who *else* should get involved. If the next step in solving the problem were, say, identifying what additional information was needed, then it could easily have been delegated to a staff member. This would better utilize the staff member's talents and also allow Terry to control the timing and content of the unexpected interruption.

In Case II, Terry chose to prepare the budget and play the role of mediator between the two faculty members. Again, a full solution is likely to require several action steps, but even if they're not fully delegated, those steps can be shared. Before simply preparing a budget report, it may have been possible for Terry to ask for additional data, examples, directions, or specific assistance from other administrators. And with the two faculty members, it might have proved productive for each of them to prepare a position statement to be shared prior to any mediation. In both cases, Terry would be giving the next action step to another person.

In Case III, the chair was being pressured by external constituents. That sort of pressure should not be avoided, as external constituents are critical to the support and success of the department. But once again, Terry's response gave someone else control of the what and when of the chair's involvement. More control could have been maintained by inviting the relevant constituents to an earlier, planned visit at the department's convenience. Even at this late date, Terry might reduce the immediacy of the request by asking for time to prepare a white paper, then scheduling a review session when more time was available.

Case IV, Terry's meeting with the dean, is a bit more delicate than the other three: it involves shifting power from someone higher in the organizational hierarchy to someone lower. When you find yourself in this position, your intent should be to take the next move; as long as you are expected to contribute to a process in which the boss decides the next move, you do not have control. For instance, Terry might determine that an appropriate next move was to prepare a written recommendation for the dean's input or approval. While this appears to do nothing but add a responsibility to the chair's already daunting list, it actually gives the chair some control over the timing and content of what the dean assigned.

Interruptions cannot be eliminated. You may not even manage to reduce them, at least in quantity. What you can reduce is their disruptive impact. By consciously determining what the next move should be and deciding who should take that next move—instead of dealing with every interruption personally—you will acquire much more control over the what and the when of your job. Don't settle for identifying your time wasters and listing how you spend each day. More importantly, focus on:

1. Deciding the content and timing of the next move,

2. Deciding who should be responsible for that move (putting the "monkey" on the right back), and

3. Placing all the moves in the right context (coordinating action steps instead of delegating everything).

Review the concept of the management molecule (Figure 5.1) and determine who, in your department, plays each role. With this in mind, recall an unexpected interruption you experienced during the past few days and identify where it originated on your management molecule. Then analyze who controlled the timing and content of your reaction to the interruption.

Using Exercise 5.1, identify what should have been done, and by whom. Then generate several alternatives for *assigning* the next move (if the interruption involved a colleague or member of your support staff) or *taking* the next move (if the interruption involved the dean).

Remember, this is not a process of delegation, it is simply a method of gaining more control over what you do and when you do it. Delegation remains an important issue, but often fails to solve the time problem. You must consciously

Exercise 5.1 Taking Control of Interruptions

Description of interruption (who, when, why): _____

_____

_____

Likely impact on management team:

    Boss (the dean): _____

    Internal others (faculty, chairs, administrators): _____

    External others (students, professionals, constituents): _____

    Subordinates (staff): _____

What immediate action(s) might be taken as a result of the interruption? _____

_____

_____

To gain control of the timing and content of your involvement, who do you believe should take the next action step? _____

_____

_____

If you have determined that *you* should take the next action step, list some ways that you, instead of the dean, might be able to bear responsibility for the next move. _____

_____

_____

If you decide to assign the next action step to the interrupting party, list some ideas for placing this responsibility with them while still preserving the relationship. _____

_____

_____

attend to who should be taking the next action step(s) and review your alternatives for getting them assigned to the right person(s).

Formal meetings

Note what managers, directors, and other administrators have to say about meetings: "There are too many meetings; many meetings are with the wrong people; too many meetings are poorly run; meetings typically last too long and frequently lack sufficient follow-up; the average manager spends nearly ten hours a week in meetings, and 90 percent of managers say that over half of their meetings are wasted time" (Mackenzie 1990, 136). In some meeting-prone fields, like education, the total is even higher. Department chairs have meetings—lots of them. Your challenge will be to make your department meetings more effective, and to consciously reduce the number of other meetings you attend.

Reducing the number of meetings you attend outside your department is relatively easy, but not automatic. Making a conscious, rather than reflexive, choice each time you are invited to attend another meeting can assist you. One helpful strategy is considering whether attendance at a given meeting fits into your management molecule. Will it make a difference to those on your management team? If you are invited to attend a meeting that will not impact your dean (the boss), your department employees (staff), your faculty and university colleagues (internal others), or other department stakeholders (external others), then you should probably decline the opportunity.

Even when the invited meetings involve your management team, you should determine, 1) the purpose of the meeting and those who will participate in it, 2) your role in the meeting's agenda, and 3) the start-time and duration of the meeting. You can then base your decision on the value of your time in relation to the purpose of the meeting and your relationship to the other attendees. You must also decide whether the length of the meeting is commensurate with the meeting's purpose and your relationship to those invited. Finally, you can determine whether it would be feasible to attend only the portion of the meeting that is pertinent to your management team, and, if so, give proper notice. With these few simple—but far from automatic—decisions, your time spent in unnecessary meetings can be reduced.

Exercise 5.2 will help you cut down on the number of meetings you attend outside your department. Identify one external meeting that you plan to attend in the near future and use the checklist to determine whether you should attend and, if you should, whether you should stay for the entirety.

When it comes to your own department meetings, there are three ways to dramatically minimize unproductive time. First, question whether the meeting should be held. What is your intent? Is it to share or exchange ideas, to gather additional information for a decision, or to build relationships with and motivate those in attendance? Once you have defined the specific purpose of the

84

Exercise 5.2 Choosing Meetings

External meeting to be considered: _____

Relationship of this meeting and its invited participants to your management team:

    Boss (the dean): _____

    Internal others (faculty, chairs, administrators): _____

    External others (students, professionals, constituents): _____

    Subordinates (staff): _____

Stated meeting purpose: _____

Your specific role or purpose in attending this meeting: _____

Based on the above considerations, note the time and duration of your commitment:

    ___ Attend full meeting

    ___ Attend part of the meeting (which part?) _____

    ___ Not attend the meeting

Completing this simple assessment when deciding whether to attend an external meeting can save you time without costing you needed information or important contacts.

---

meeting, ask yourself if a meeting is really the best way to accomplish it. Might it be achieved satisfactorily with an email or phone call to all participants? Is it actually necessary to get everyone together, or could individual information be conveyed more selectively?

Second, establish the length of time needed for the meeting to accomplish your purpose. A beginning and an ending time should be communicated to all invited, and that schedule should be kept. An agenda should be prepared in advance and shared with all participants (with time limits for each topic and required decisions noted). You might want to designate a staff member the official timekeeper. This will allow you to make time adjustments in a non-threatening, impersonal manner.

Third, carefully determine who should attend each meeting. Inviting everyone so you won't offend anyone usually results in offending several who are invited without their wanting or needing to be there. As you consider who should be invited, the Vroom-Yetton participative-decision-making model may be helpful; according to this model, deciding who to invite to a meeting should rely on four factors:

1. *Is the outcome of this meeting important to the department?*

   If your answer is "not really," the meeting is probably unnecessary.

2. *Is additional information needed? If so, who has access to that information?*

   If only certain people have the information you need, you will naturally want to be sure those people are invited. If the information is readily available to you, you might substitute one-on-one encounters for a meeting.

3. *Are those likely to be influenced by the meeting's outcome likely to understand and accept that outcome?*

   If the answer is yes, then the necessity of the meeting will be determined mainly by what information you need. If the answer is no, you may need to hold a meeting to encourage consensus, or at least understanding—even if additional information is not needed.

4. *Is there likely to be significant disagreement among those affected by the meeting's topic?*

   If conflict is likely, a meeting will be helpful. As will be discussed in chapter 6, bringing up differences when all parties are present is an important first step in resolving those differences. That said, some parties to the conflict may not have the department's best interests in mind. Therefore, a meeting, while helpful, should not give the group the power to make a binding decision. Discussions are important and information is necessary to resolve disagreements, but when individuals' self-interests are at odds, the chair should clearly have the final say (Vroom and Jago 1988).

Faculty/staff interactions

It is not a problem to spend time with your faculty and staff. In fact, this is your most vital role. Don't try to eliminate or even reduce it. Your staff and faculty are the very essence of your job. Relieving your time crunch shouldn't lead to fewer interactions with them: it should lead to fewer unplanned, unproductive interactions. The best way to improve your interactions with faculty and staff is to welcome them, enjoy them, and keep them focused on the goals and mission of your department. Whether you are evaluating performance, resolving differences, providing motivation and direction, or soliciting ideas and suggestions, follow the examples found in chapters 2–4. Your departmental interactions need not be reduced, but they can be made more cohesive and productive as you promote individual achievement and encourage personal action plans toward the department's mission and key outcomes. To better enjoy your time with staff and faculty, be sure to establish and communicate a clear department mission. Take some time to identify the key outcomes for your depart-

---

Exercise 5.3 Departmental Meeting Planning Form

Purpose of meeting:

QUESTION #1: How important are the decisions or outcomes of this meeting to those on your management team:
After considering this question, do you still want to schedule this meeting?
___ Yes ___ No

QUESTION #2: Do you have sufficient information for the purpose of this meeting? If not, do you know who has the needed information?
If you have the necessary information, you may want to handle this with a memo or individual phone calls.

If you need additional information, list those on your team who are likely to have it:

_____ _____ _____ _____

_____ _____ _____ _____

QUESTION #3: Are those on your management team likely to understand and accept the decision or other outcomes from this meeting without participating? ___ Yes ___ No

If not, you will want to include those members of your team whose understanding and acceptance is particularly important:

_____ _____ _____ _____

_____ _____ _____ _____

QUESTION #4: Are there likely to be different opinions among those on your management team? ___ Yes ___ No

If so, list those between whom a conflict will need to be aired:

_____ _____ _____ _____

_____ _____ _____ _____

For more productive sessions, you may want to invite only those people you have listed above.

Based on the above considerations, make a list of those appropriate to invite to the meeting:

_____ _____ _____ _____

_____ _____ _____ _____

ment and communicate the short-term goals that will build those outcomes. Remain aware of how the faculty relate to the goals, and how the goals relate to your vision.

Personal decisions

The first step in resolving your time problems—perhaps the only step really required—is recognizing and accepting that *you* are both the problem and the solution. "Time management" is really a misnomer. Time is a constant. Every day has the same number of hours. You can't manage time as though it were something separate and malleable; what you can do is manage your *relationship* to time.

Consider the following example: A graduate student in business administration complained of a severe time problem. She was failing one class and performing below average in two others. Her specific complaint was that she simply did not have enough time to succeed in all three classes. A brief discussion revealed that the real problem was a fiancé who had just moved into the area. The student suggested an interesting solution: she asked if her professor would help her get control of her schedule. She prepared a strict daily study regimen and asked for it to be posted publicly. She then checked in every day with the professor to enforce her adherence to the schedule.

The days didn't get longer, no one else's behavior changed, but the results were dramatic. Grades in all three classes rose to above average, and the student still had time to spend with her fiancé. While she wasn't initially able to solve her time problem, she did take the initiative in seeking assistance. Control, not time, was the problem and the solution.

Your choices make the difference. If you can't seem to solve time problems, create a system or seek out assistance in regaining your ability to choose the what and when of your professional life. While in one sense the graduate student gave away her control, she ultimately acquired a level of control she hadn't had, and the choices remained with her.

It is not uncommon for department chairs to incur serious demands on their time as a result of taking on too many responsibilities. Mackenzie stated that this problem often occurs "because we simply do not know what to say in difficult situations, so we end up saying yes when we didn't want to, we allow other people to interrupt us because we don't want to offend them, we accept confusing instructions from the boss because we don't want to appear stupid...and we end up falling further and further behind" (1990). The solution is not more time; it is more control over what you choose to do and when you choose to do it.

## Chapter 6

MANAGING CONFLICT CREATIVELY

Valuing Diverse Perspectives

> You cannot shake hands with a closed fist.
> — Golda Meir

Higher education scholars and practitioners propose that the department chair hovers between faculty and administration. At best, the chair stands with one foot in each camp and shifts his or her weight from one foot to the other, depending on the situation. With this in mind, consider your sense of orientation on the continuum below, from faculty at 1 to administration at 7.

Faculty 1   2   3   4   5   6   7   Administration

Where did you place yourself? When eight hundred department chairs responded, the majority found themselves somewhere in the middle (55 percent answered 3, 4, or 5), with only 6 percent administratively oriented and 29 percent faculty oriented.

Caught between the conflicting interests of faculty and administration, department chairs often don't know which way to turn. While mediating the concerns of administration and faculty, they try to champion the values of their faculty. As a result, they find themselves swiveling between their faculty colleagues and the administration. In essence, they are caught in the role of Janus, the Roman god with two faces looking in different directions at the same time. Chairs don't have to worry about being deified, but they do find themselves between a rock and a hard place: chairs are at the heart of the tension between two potentially different value systems. Conflict is inherent in their position, and they suffer from it. They must learn to swivel between administration and faculty without appearing dizzy, schizophrenic, or two-faced.

DEPARTMENT CHAIR CONFLICT-MOLECULE

Results are mixed on who within the academy suffers the most conflict. Our research leads us to conclude that department chairs, caught as they are in the middle, constantly find themselves in conflict situations (Gmelch and Miskin 2004; Wolverton and Gmelch 2002). Already viewed as neither fish nor fowl (faculty nor administration), the department chair, as represented in Figure 6.1, finds that the demands from above typically conflict with those from below.

Department chairs find themselves saddled with incompatible expectations and subjected to role conflict between the dean and faculty (see Higgerson 1996; Higgerson and Joyce 2007; Gmelch and Sarros 1996). For example, they must contend with expectations from the dean to cut costs, while dealing with faculty who demand more travel funds, instructional materials, and research dollars to maintain their expected productivity. As chairs look above and below to assess the expectations placed upon them, they must not forget to look to the sides—to their peers and outsiders.

On the left side of the molecule, chairs feel pressure from their constituents: students, agencies, and alumni. Consequently, they may feel boxed in from all sides without enough time, resources, or reason to resolve the conflict. Although this chapter focuses on the resolution of chair-faculty conflict, the conflict-resolution techniques introduced are not unique to any one relationship in the conflict molecule.

A study conducted by the Center for the Study of the Department Chair found, not surprisingly, that chairs identified conflict with colleagues as their foremost source of stress (Gmelch et al 1992). As noted in Table 6.1, over 40 percent of the department chairs suffered excessive stress from "making decisions affecting others, resolving collegial differences, and evaluating faculty performance" (see chapter 7). In contrast, only seventeen percent of the chairs complained of excessive stress from resolving differences with deans, while 5 percent reported excessive stress from resolving conflicts with students. Overall, no other activities produced as much stress as chairs' responsibilities to faculty.

CONFLICT AND DISSATISFACTION

Chairs also described when they felt most dissatisfied with their jobs. Second only to bureaucratic red tape and paperwork was the chairs' frustration

Figure 6.1 Department Chair Conflict-Molecule

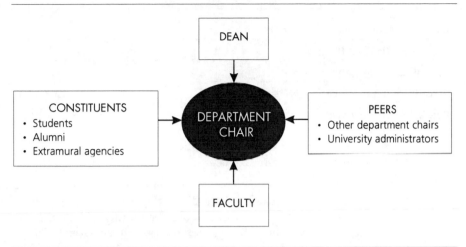

with interpersonal conflict. Sixty percent of their dissatisfaction came from dealing with faculty involved in the following types of conflict:

1. *Inter-faculty conflict.* Most of the chairs' dissatisfaction came from faculty disagreeing with each other, which resulted in "bickering, whining, and feuding," "acting without reason," and "ideological and personal wars."

2. *Faculty attitude.* Chairs felt disappointed when faculty were seen as "unimaginative, apathetic, disengaged," colleagues who were "recalcitrant and no longer focused on the mission," and "[did] not measure up to their potential."

3. *Unsupportive faculty.* Another source of conflict surfaced when faculty did not support the direction of the department: "chairs dealing with faculty resistance to improvements and change," "faculty acting unreasonably (and selfishly), thereby causing turmoil and compromising the achievement of departmental objectives," and "when interpersonal differences between faculty inhibit the mission of the department and . . . basically work against the good of the department."

4. *Unsupportive chair.* Chairs also expressed remorse when they could not support their faculty; i.e., had to "make decisions which cause great disappointment to [their] colleagues," and "when [they] can't, or don't, have the resources to reward good faculty."

5. *Role of evaluation.* Although evaluation is inherent in their role, chairs reported difficulty in having to "evaluate their colleagues,"

Table 6.1 Chair Confrontational Stressors

Making decisions affecting others	45%
Resolving collegial differences	45%
Evaluating faculty performance	42%
Resolving differences with superiors	17%
Resolving differences with students	5%

"conduct annual reviews," "make tough decisions on merit evaluations and salaries," and "fire faculty."

6. *Role of mediation*. Finally, chairs' role in mediating conflict between their colleagues caused them dissatisfaction. One chair expressed concern over "severe faculty confrontations," and another expressed difficulty "when I have to referee bad interpersonal relations between faculty."

The remaining 40 percent of conflict situations causing chair dissatisfaction stemmed from dealing with higher-level administration—the top of the conflict-molecule in Figure 6.1. Chairs reported on the "frustration from lack of support" or "unresponsiveness from higher administration," and "when higher-up administrators do not share information upon which decisions affecting my department are made." Another concern came from chairs' frustration when "higher administration requires what seems to be excessive paperwork," or "unrealistic deadlines," and "requesting reports that are never responded to." Finally, chairs felt conflict with higher-level administrators when they had opposing values, when they felt unappreciated for work done or successes delivered, and when their recommendations or input were not accepted.

All these forces place department chairs in a difficult position. In order to foresee and respond effectively to crises and pressures, chairs need to be equipped with creative conflict management skills. The following focuses on the skills necessary to help chairs recognize, respond to, and resolve conflicts within academe.

APPROACHES TO CONFLICT MANAGEMENT

When you think of conflict, what is the first word that comes to mind? Most chairs develop images of controversy, of disagreement, of differing opinions between faculty members. While negative images may predominate, conflict is not necessarily undesirable. Emotional responses to conflict can be positive (e.g., excitement, enjoyment, stimulation, curiosity, creativity, commitment, involvement), negative (e.g., anger, distrust, resentment, fear, rejection), or even neutral (e.g., change, or a different point of view).

Table 6.2 Approaches to Organizational Conflict

PERIOD	PHILOSOPHY	NATURE	PRESCRIPTION STRATEGY
1890s–1940s	Traditional	Destructive	Eliminate
1950s–1980s	Behavioral	Natural	Accept
Present	Principled	Necessary	Encourage

One of management's main functions is to adjudicate conflicting demands. How should you, as chair, view conflict within your department? The answer rests in your basic philosophical approach. As seen in Table 6.2, managerial attitudes toward conflict can be segregated into three categories: traditional, behavioral, and principled. The first two philosophies comprise views historically held in the management literature (Robbins 1974), and the third proposes a new way to handle conflict.

Traditional

The traditionalists' approach from the late nineteenth century through the mid-1940s was simple: conflict was destructive and should therefore be eliminated. The role of the manager was to purge conflict from the organization. In higher education, the traditionalist chair believed that conflict should be thoroughly analyzed, suppressed, and eliminated—it was destructive and should be avoided (Williams 1985). Naturally, exceptions to this generalization existed, but the bottom line seemed to be that conflict created ill dispositions rather than constructive dialogue.

Behavioral

By the 1950s, the behavioral view gained traction in the literature and in practice. Freud believed that aggressiveness was an innate, independent, instinctual disposition of people; we should accept conflict as natural and inevitable, since "complex organizations, by their very nature, have built-in conflicts. Disagreements over goals clearly exist. Sections compete for recognition. Departments compete for prestige. . . . All compete for power" (Robbins 1974, 13). As management guru Warren Bennis points out: "Conflicts stem basically from differences among persons and groups. Elimination of conflict would mean the elimination of such differences. The goal of conflict management is, for us, better conceived as the acceptance and enhancement of differences among persons and groups . . ." (Bennis, Benne, and Chin 1969, 152). Conflict is inevitable, so the chair's strategy should be to manage it. However, managing conflict because it is inevitable does not go far enough. In order to tap the real benefit of conflict, it should at times be promoted as an avenue for exploring common grounds, interests, and mutual benefits—which leads to the third philosophy of conflict management.

Principled

By the 1980s, conflict management had entered into what has been termed a "principled approach." Principled conflict management promotes integrity and high standards, such that all parties exhibit righteousness, uprightness, and trustworthiness in attempting to resolve differences. With principled conflict management, the use of "tricky tactics" is abandoned for a more honest, open approach—an approach that conceives of conflict as a necessary and encouraged condition of administration. It cultivates diverse perspectives in the hope of finding new, creative solutions. In the 1970s, a review of managerial practices found few administrators employing principled philosophy (Robbins 1974). However, over the past decade, successful administrators have begun to recognize that, in many instances, conflict signals a healthy academic organization (Gunsalus 2006). The recent popularity of the Harvard Negotiation Project (Fisher and Ury 1983) has influenced an even broader use of principled conflict resolution.

This chapter discusses the ingredients necessary for principled resolution. The three R's of principled conflict management (recognize, respond, and resolve) are presented here with the following objectives in mind:

1. *Recognize* the nature and causes of conflict;

2. Identify and explore effective *response* options; and

3. Practice the art of principled conflict *resolution*.

Conflict Recognition

Your first step toward a positive and constructive conflict management style is to recognize the nature and causes of conflict in your department, and in the university or college as a whole. Unfortunately, most people take conflict personally. Some chairs feel that conflict, whatever its reason, is their fault. However, even though chairs may not like to talk about conflict, they need to accept the idea that it occurs; when it comes to such complex organizations as universities and colleges, conflict is sewn into the institutional fabric.

A review of the research on organizational conflict reveals ten structural relationships that create conflict among faculty and administrators, regardless of the particular people involved. It is important to recognize that these tensions do not originate with individuals. Rather, they are part of the institution's architecture.

To assess the nature of conflicts in your department and institution more specifically, take a moment to answer the ten questions in Exercise 6.1. Remember, not all conflict is negative or unnecessary.

Exercise 6.1 Department Chair Working Conditions

Indicate where your department or college/university falls on the scales

1. ORGANIZATIONAL STRUCTURE:

relatively flat organization	1	2	3	4	5	6	7	formal hierarchy (6–7 levels)

2. DEGREE OF AUTHORITY:

informal/ autonomy	1	2	3	4	5	6	7	Routiniaztion & rules & regulation

3. DEGREE OF SPECIALIZATION:

low job specialiation	1	2	3	4	5	6	7	high job specialization

4. STAFF COMPOSITION:

homogeneous facuty & staff	1	2	3	4	5	6	7	heterogeneous faculty & staff

5. MANAGERIAL SUPERVISION:

loose/ autonomous supervision	1	2	3	4	5	6	7	close supervision

6. DEPARTMENTAL DECISION MAKING:

democratic	1	2	3	4	5	6	7	autocratic

7. SOURCE OF POWER:

personal power	1	2	3	4	5	6	7	positional power

8. REWARD AND RECOGNITION:

abundant rewards & resources	1	2	3	4	5	6	7	Limited rewards & resources

9. INTERDEPENDENCE AMONG WORK UNITS:

autonomous independent units	1	2	3	4	5	6	7	interconnected dependent units

10. ROLES AND RESPONSIBILITIES

faculty-oriented	1	2	3	4	5	6	7	administration-oriented

Total your score and find it below:
50–70 . . . . High conflict   30–49 . . . . Moderate conflict
10–29 . . . . Low conflict   0–9 . . . . . . Minimal conflict

The following ten summaries of the research explain the basis of the questions in Exercise 6.1; they will give you insight into both your score and the nature of conflict in colleges and universities.

1. *Levels.* Most would agree that as the size of an organization increases, goals become less clear, interpersonal relationships become more formal, departments become more specialized, and the potential for conflict intensifies. These common-sense assumptions have been supported by research in educational organizations. Specifically, Corwin found that 83 percent of schools with six or seven levels of authority reported high rates of disagreement between faculty and administrators, as opposed to 14 percent in schools with three or fewer levels of authority (1969). Not unexpectedly, as the administrative line-authority in universities increases, the potential for conflict between the echelons also increases. How many levels can you count in your university or college? Even more importantly, what do you perceive to be the psychological and sociological distance between each level—i.e., how high is your hierarchy?

2. *Rules and regulations.* Generally, as job structure increases, the amount of role certainty increases, thus reducing *inter*personal conflict between employees. However, with increased job structure, employees also feel greater *intra*personal role conflict: they become confined by routinization, rules, and regulations. In higher education, where faculty have a great deal of autonomy, the potential for interpersonal conflict increases, as roles become less clear and more difficult to monitor and supervise. On the flip side, this autonomy reduces potential intrapersonal conflict. Are you and your faculty governed by tight rules, regulations, and job definitions? If so, you can expect less interpersonal conflict with your colleagues, but greater conflict within individuals who have fewer places to go and grow.

3. *Degree of specialization.* In a study of schools, high degrees of specialization increased the intensity of conflict. Secondary schools segmented into departments suffer more conflict than homogeneous elementary schools. Higher education institutions with departments housed in separate buildings experience more conflict than secondary schools. This does not, of course, mean that elementary schools offer better working environments than colleges; conflict can generate positive outcomes. Nevertheless, if the departments within your college are highly specialized and relatively autonomous, you may find them in competition for common resources.

4. *Staff composition.* Well-established groups have been found to develop more constructive conflict than ad hoc committees (Hall and Williams 1966). Therefore, one would expect high staff turnover to stimulate conflict within organizations (Robbins 1974). Professionals in higher education tend to be less mobile than their counterparts in the business sector, and their stability may be a factor in reduced departmental conflicts. What proportion of your faculty are tenured and stable? You should consider not only longevity but differences in age, gender, background, values, and other demographic and psychosocial factors that influence interpersonal conflict. For example, as both age and tenure increase among staff members, the degree of conflict decreases. While a homogeneous staff may experience less interpersonal conflict than a heterogeneous group, the conflict generated from the diversity of the mixed group may result in productive and healthy changes. If you have an established, homogeneous faculty you may have less conflict than more diverse departments—but are your faculty meetings challenging and productive?

5. *Nature of supervision.* The more closely someone is supervised, the more conflict will be created. This doesn't mean that close supervision is never warranted. If change is required in employee behavior, then close supervision may be necessary and lead to positive results. On the other hand, faculty in higher education plan and control their own work and work styles, and as long as they produce the desired results in teaching, research, and service, the tension produced by close supervision is unnecessary. Do you give your productive faculty the supportive autonomy they need, and your struggling faculty more guidance?

6. *Participation in decision making.* Faculty assume involvement in departmental decision making. Interestingly, as the level of participation increases, the amount of conflict also increases. Most studies support the conclusion that participation in decision making and conflict are positively correlated. This is especially true where value differences exist, as will be noted in the section of this chapter on resolution. The assumption behind participatory decision making is that the quality of the decisions will increase with more input. While this may be true in most cases, there are definitely tradeoffs in time, efficiency, and effectiveness.

7. *Sources of power.* French and Raven (1968) suggest five bases of social power: department chairs can influence faculty through the authority vested in the position (legitimate power), through their ability to provide rewards and recognition (reward power), through their ability to punish and to withhold rewards (coercive

power), through their knowledge and skills (expertise power), and through personal persuasion (referent power). Summaries of research indicate that the use of expertise and referent power (personal sources) yields greater satisfaction and performance than coercive power (Yukl 1981). Normative organizations such as universities and colleges rely predominantly on symbols, rather than coercion or financial rewards, to influence employees. Leaders in these organizations, department chairs in particular, wield informal control by virtue of their personalities and positions. In fact, "low and moderate levels of power . . . can assist in improving coordination and, therefore, work to reduce conflict. But where power is excessive, as perceived by a less powerful group, one may expect it to be challenged, causing increased conflict" (Robbins 1974, 48).

In higher education, faculty hold exceptional power through their professionalism; their expertise critically contributes to the success or failure of the department. You, as chair, must recognize these sources of power and use them wisely. Power decisions should be made on the basis of department productivity, not on the expectations of conflict.

8. *Rewards and recognition.* Rewards and recognition also contribute significantly to conflict. When different reward structures are used for different groups or departments, conflict is likely to occur. In other words, the more rewards emphasize separate performance, rather than combined performance, the greater the conflict (Walton and Dutton 1969). This relationship is even more pronounced if the groups perceive that they are competing for the same or limited resources, e.g., if you must divide a fixed sum of merit-increases among your faculty, you will likely encounter conflict between and among colleagues.

9. *Interdependence.* In much the way that conflict is created by different systems of reward and recognition, the more faculty must rely on each other, or one department rely on another department, or one academic course build on another to complete a task or gain achievement, the more conflict will increase. In his definitive work on conflict, sociologist Georg Simmel concludes that conflict will occur when the activities of one individual or group have a direct consequence on another's ability to achieve its goal (1955).

10. *Roles and responsibilities.* Managers, who perform liaison or linkage roles in organizations, often find themselves in role-conflict situations (Kahn et al 1964). Academic department chairs encounter even greater role conflict, since they are in a somewhat unique position that lacks common management parallels. Researchers have

found that department chairs are plagued with inherent structural conflict, due to acting as the conduit of information and policy between the administration and the faculty of the institution (Lee 1985; Milstein 1987). The ambiguity and role conflict results from attempting to bridge the administrative and academic cores of the university, which are organized and operated differently (Bare 1986). The academic core of teaching and research operates freely and independently in a loosely coupled system, whereas the managerial core maintains the mechanistic qualities of a tightly coupled system. Department chairs are at the heart of the tension between the two systems. While the dynamic conflict between administration and academics is critical to maintaining higher education organizations, it may cause chairs to feel trapped between the pressure to perform as a faculty member and the pressure to perform as an administrator. These pressures, unique to department chairs, force them to maintain a difficult balance: mimicking the two-faced Janus without succumbing to hypocrisy.

In summary, a review of the research in educational institutions reveals ten work relationships that inevitably increase the intensity of conflict among colleagues. It is not difficult to see that institutions of higher education have conflict embedded in their many levels, their rules and regulations, their specialized disciplines, their heterogeneous staffing, their participatory decision making, their segmented rewards, their high degree of interdependence, their use of authoritative positional power, and their tension between the academic and administrative core of faculty and administration.

The purpose of this section is not to outline a debate on whether structural conflict is good or bad, but for you to recognize that conflict exists, need not be avoided, and should not to be taken personally. We move now to the second "R" of conflict management: the need to *respond* appropriately when conflict arises. As chair, you need to realize that regardless of the causes, your response to conflict situations is your personal responsibility.

CONFLICT RESPONSE

Having identified the nature and causes of conflict in your department, now devote your attention to your options for response. The pioneering work of Kenneth W. Thomas (1976) provides a theoretical construct and a human-relations instrument with which to test the practical application of individuals' response options (Thomas and Kilmann 1974). Basically, think of your response options as organized along two behavioral dimensions: 1) how *assertive* you are in terms of trying to satisfy your own concerns and interests, and 2) how *cooperative* you are in terms of satisfying the interests and concerns of others. Different proportions of strength and weakness along these two dimensions can be

Figure 6.2 Conflict Management

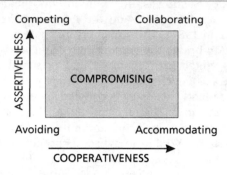

configured as five conflict-response styles, as displayed in Figure 6.2. Much of the following discussion is based on the original work of Thomas and Kilmann, which we have adapted to the potential conflict between department chairs and faculty (1974).

1. *Competition* (high assertiveness and low cooperativeness). In this response style you would choose to pursue your own interests or your department's interests at the expense of staff or faculty. This is a power-oriented mode in which all power sources (both positional and personal) would be used. It would require you to use your ability of persuasion, academic rank, position, or reward and punishment to win.

2. *Accommodation* (low assertiveness and high cooperativeness). The opposite of competition is accommodation, where neglect of your own or the department's concerns may be necessary to satisfy faculty needs. This self-sacrificial response may take the form of yielding to faculty points of view, giving personal time to promote the needs of faculty, or being altruistic in dealing with faculty concerns.

3. *Avoidance* (low assertiveness and low cooperativeness). In the event you choose not to address issues, and neither assert nor cooperate, you are avoiding confrontation. You may choose this response to sidestep an issue, postpone it until later, or withdraw from it completely.

4. *Compromise* (intermediate assertiveness and intermediate cooperativeness). A compromise response style seeks an immediate, mutually acceptable solution that partially satisfies you and your faculty. Rather than striving for the best solution, compromise centers on

the resolution of conflict by splitting the difference, exchanging resources, or seeking a middle position.

5. *Collaboration* (high assertiveness and high cooperativeness). Collaboration is the ideal response to conflict between you and your
faculty. Given time and cooperation, you can satisfy your own interests and concerns as well as those of your department and faculty.
But, as you are well aware, time and cooperation *are* required.

Before addressing resolution, several points should be made about conflict
responses. First, seldom is a single option chosen: a blend of all five response
styles is often the best path to a final resolution. Second, collaboration is not always the most effective or efficient response style. Finally, many advantages and
disadvantages can be ascribed to each response style on a situation-by-situation
basis. The question is not which is the best style, but which is the right style for
a particular situation. Figure 6.3 outlines the advantages and disadvantages of
each conflict style. Competition is useful when you need quick action, and
when protection is needed against faculty who take advantage of nonassertive
behavior. You may wish to accommodate when an issue is of little importance
to you, or when it is important to build relationships with faculty. Avoidance
may be useful when you believe the risks of conflict clearly outweigh the gains,
or when more information is needed. When an expedient solution is needed in
order to resolve time pressure, compromise may temporarily be your best bet.
Finally, you should include your faculty in a collaborative effort when an issue is
too important to compromise or when new, permanent solutions are required.

In summary, the effectiveness of a response style depends on the conditions of the conflict situation. One style is not always better than another; chairs
and faculty should have enough flexibility, skill, and comfort to use any of the
five styles. Rather than discuss style preference, you need to assess which style
produces the desired resolution and builds the desired relationships.

The framework of Thomas and Kilmann can be extended by asking two
basic questions: 1) Is the *substantive outcome* very important to the manager?
2) Is the *relationship outcome* very important to the manager? These two questions can help you decide which style best suits your needs. The first question
relates to assertiveness (importance of outcome), the vertical axis of Figure 6.2.
The second question relates to the horizontal axis, cooperativeness (importance of relationship). Figure 6.4 maps the conflict resolution strategies you
should consider based on what aspect of the outcome is most important to you.

1. Use the strategy of *collaboration* when both relationships and substantive outcomes are important. Openness between you and your
faculty will be crucial in achieving a win-win outcome.

2. If you are more concerned with establishing a positive relationship
with your faculty than with realizing substantive goals, then *accom-*

Figure 6.3 Selecting Appropriate Conflict Responses

COMPETITION		COLLABORATION	
Advantages	Disadvantages	Advantages	Disadvantages
• Useful when quick action is required • Protects against those who take advantage of non-competitive behavior	• Stops exploration of new approaches • One's goals may be achieved at the expense of others • Win/lose • Little commitment • Temporary solution	• Mutual exploration of new approaches • Mutual resolution • Fains commitment • Win/win • Permanent solution	• Can be time consuming • Requires participation from others

COMPROMISE

AVOIDANCE		ACCOMMODATION	
Advantages	Disadvantages	Advantages	Disadvantages
• Useful when risk outweighs gains • Postpones tension • Useful when others can solve the problem more effectively • Useful to postpone action until more information surfaces	• Restricts input • Temporary solution	• Useful to preserve harmony • Avoids disruptions • Prevents competition • Useful when issues are not important to you	• Sacrifices your own point of view • Limits creative resolution • Win/lose

ASSERTIVE

Dominant

Submissive

← Non-Supportive   Supportive →

COOPERATIVE

Figure 6.4 Conflict Resolution Strategies

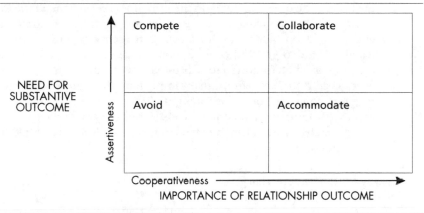

NEED FOR
SUBSTANTIVE
OUTCOME

Assertiveness

| Compete | Collaborate |
| Avoid | Accommodate |

Cooperativeness ————————————————————→
IMPORTANCE OF RELATIONSHIP OUTCOME

modation will be more appropriate. This is a yield-win strategy that allows relationships to be strengthened at cost to outcomes.

3. *Competition* is called for when substantive goals are of more concern than relationships. Use this strategy when you have little trust in your faculty, or when faculty interests are detrimental to departmental goals or outcomes. You end up with a win-lose solution.

4. If neither substantive outcomes nor relationships are important to you, *avoidance* allows you to withdraw from the issue. It should not be your default strategy, but is useful when you believe the conflict can be resolved without intervention, or when you need time or additional information.

These four strategies open up a proactive dimension of conflict resolution. Presumably, department chairs strive to maintain positive relationships with their faculty members; they should therefore seek a *resolution* that preserves the best interests of all parties—bringing us to the third and final "R" of conflict management.

CONFLICT RESOLUTION

The final "R" of creative conflict management is the search for a long-term *resolution* that satisfies both parties' interests and concerns. In preparation for long-term solutions, some time for analysis is important. Answering the questions below can provide you with a framework for analyzing the conflict situation (Raiffa 1982).

1. *Are there more than two parties?* Visualize yourself sitting across the table from the chair of another department, discussing the pos-

sibility of merging a program in one department with a program in the other. The question here: do the two of you represent all the interests and concerns that need consideration, or are other constituencies lined up behind each of you, representing your "vertical teams" (Figure 6.5)? While both of you may agree on the terms of a merger, have you forgotten to consult your vertical teams—i.e., the faculty, staff, students, and, equally important, the alumni, who represent a powerful force for tradition? Before you enter an agreement with another chair or anyone else, consider the vertical teams behind each of you and analyze what interests of theirs are enfolded in the decision.

Figure 6.5 The Vertical Team

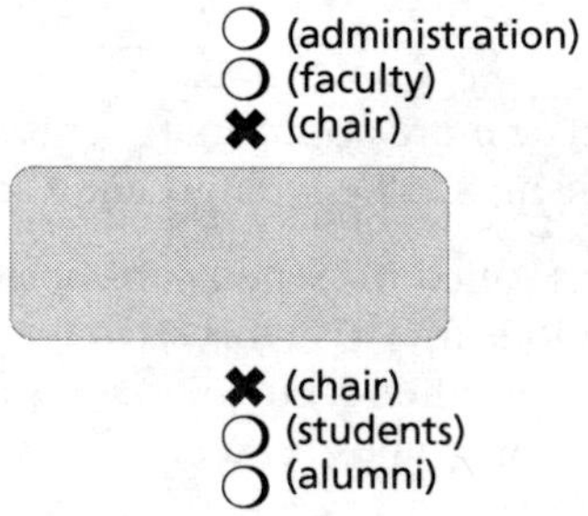

⚪ (administration)
⚪ (faculty)
✖ (chair)

✖ (chair)
⚪ (students)
⚪ (alumni)

2. *Are the parties monolithic?* It is probably the rule that both sides of a dispute are not internally monolithic. This question addresses your "horizontal team," the person figuratively sitting next to you on your side of the table (Figure 6.6). Do the two of you form a monolithic body of interests? Probably not. Take the classic case of the defending attorney and client. Both want to resolve the dispute, but the client's interest may be in resolving it immediately so as to take care of bills and tackle other pursuits. The attorney, who may be paid by billable hours or a percentage of the settlement, may want to hold out for a bigger payday.

Figure 6.6 Horizontal Team

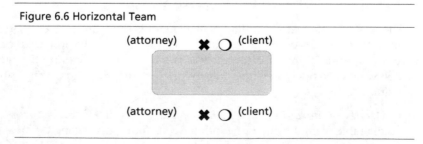

(attorney)   ✖ ⚪   (client)

(attorney)   ✖ ⚪   (client)

3. *Are there linkage effects?* One agreement may have an effect on another. If you agree, based on certain principles, to dispense funds for one faculty member's professional travel, the same principles should be used to assess the next request. Your decisions, therefore, should be based on sound and defensible principles.

4. *Is there more than one issue?* Confrontations with multiple issues require trade-offs and often present difficult analytical problems. If multiple issues exist, develop a hierarchy from which you can analyze each issue against another and make your trade-offs.

5. *Is ratification among faculty required?* Make sure that if conflict about the alternative solutions is likely and you have goal congruence, your decision should be taken to faculty for ratification or endorsement.

6. *Are threats possible?* While physical threats are highly unlikely, recognize that tenured faculty have a great deal of power and can make your job very uncomfortable.

7. *Are negotiations public or private?* What you say in an open faculty meeting has much more impact than what you negotiate with someone behind closed doors. Choose your words carefully in public forums, as you may lose face if you are forced to reverse your decision.

8. *Is there a time constraint or time-related cost?* Clearly, the closer you are to a deadline (e.g., a contract or the start of an academic year), the more powerful the need to resolve the issue. To use an extreme example, when the North Vietnamese delegation arrived in Paris to seek a settlement to the Vietnam War, they rented a house on a two-year lease and let that fact be known. The party who has to negotiate in haste is disadvantaged.

Answering these questions can help you reach a wise and thoughtful settlement. Analysis is essential to effective conflict-resolution. Exercise 6.2 prompts you to use the eight basic organizing questions to analyze predicaments in your department. You will find that if you use these questions to prepare for critical conflict situations, it will be easier to be principled in your approach.

PRINCIPLED CONFLICT RESOLUTION

Overall, chairs must take care that the *relationship outcome* between them and their faculties is not indiscriminately sacrificed to the benefit of a *substantive outcome*. Fisher and Ury of the Harvard Negotiation Project discovered methods to confirm and expand this rule of thumb (1983). They suggest that

---

Exercise 6.2 Organizing Questions for Conflict Framework Development

---

Recall a conflict scenario you have addressed in your department. Analyze its key points according to the following eight organizing questions.

1. Are there more than two parties involved in this case? If so, identify them and develop a vertical team diagram (Figure 6.5).

2. Are the individuals on each side of this issue monolithic in their interests? If not, outline their separate interests and develop a horizontal team diagram (Figure 6.6).

3. Are there linkage effects?

4. Is more than one issue involved in this decision? If so, outline the issues and rank them to consider the proper trade-offs.

5. Is approval of the decision required by the faculty?

6. Are faculty threats possible? If so, identify them and how you might defuse them.

7. Have the negotiations been public or private? Discuss the merits and limitations of the situation.

8. Is there a time constraint involved in this case? If so, how might you deal with this condition?

---

any method of resolution may be fairly judged by three criteria: 1) It should produce wise agreement (outcome), 2) It should improve, or at least not damage, the relationships between the people involved, 3) It should be efficient. The first and second criteria reiterate the importance of the interplay between relationships and substance. The third criterion suggests the need to address expediency and effectiveness.

The most common form of resolution is achieved through a process of positioning and repositioning, which may or may not take into consideration the true interests of both parties. While it does communicate what is wanted and where one stands in relation to the other side, positioning fails to meet the three criteria of a wise outcome. In fact, arguing over positions produces unwise agreements, is inefficient, and endangers ongoing relationships. It is critical to understand that a wise outcome is one that "meets the legitimate interests of each side to the extent possible, resolves conflicting interests fairly, is durable, and takes community interests into account" (Fisher and Ury 1983, 4).

The technique of principled resolution, as espoused by Fisher and Ury, is a straightforward method of conflict resolution appropriate for use in almost any circumstance, especially in academic settings where both outcomes and relationships are very important to achieve and maintain. If you explore the interests, rather than the positions, of your faculty, you will build the foundation for principled conflict resolution.

Focus on interests, not positions

Focusing on positions will produce win, lose, or yield results, none of which guarantees that both parties have achieved a satisfying, long-term resolution. As outlined in Table 6.3, interests are the basic, intangible/abstract needs of a party: values, principles, and psychological or physiological needs. These are rarely talked about when parties come into conflict situations, and are also very difficult to clarify, because they are often neither negotiable nor measurable. Some of the needs normally expressed by faculty are: security, economic well-being, social acceptance, power, recognition, control, and autonomy. Promotion, tenure, and salary are all negotiable and measurable, but the personal interests of security, equity, recognition, and power are probably at the root of most faculty-chair conflicts. The bottom line is that interests must be addressed to satisfaction if conflict is to be resolved.

Reflect for a moment, refer back to the situation in Exercise 6.2, and see if you can identify what faculty interests were imbedded in the conflict situation you chose. Are you having difficulty? Use Exercise 6.3 to guide your thinking. Remember that their needs may be as basic as security (i.e., tenure) or equity (in the form of pay and rewards).

While articulating interests creates the foundation of principled resolution, three other practices provide the mortar that secures the foundation:

1. *People: Separate people from the problem.* Apropos of the demonstrations and civil disobedience of the 1950s and 1960s, Saul Alinsky's *Rules for Radicals* suggests attacking a person psychologically; once the ego gets involved, you have the advantage (1971). Principled resolution requires the opposite. You must avoid personal attacks and not impute personal feelings or concerns to others. Recognize the individual. Try to identify your faculty members' interests by actively listening and empathizing with their needs. If you become committed to a particular idea or position, your ego can get connected to your position. Your energies may then be directed toward your own defense, inclining you to attack, rather than try to solve the problem. In contrast, focusing on the problem allows the interests and perceptions of both parties to be explored without personal attacks, which can destroy relationships.

2. *Options: Generate a variety of possibilities before deciding what to do.* Avoid locking in on positions before assumptions are interrogated and interests explored. Once you and your faculty lock into your respective positions, your discussions will include only those options between position A and position B; a compromise that lies somewhere between A and B will be the only possible resolution, which means that one or both of you will lose at least partially. You will be blinded to position C, a solution that creatively satisfies ev-

---

Table 6.3 Exploring Faculty Interests

DEFINITION

Interests: the basic intangible or abstract needs of faculty, such as values, principles, or needs.

CHARACTERISTICS

Rarely negotiable

Usually intangible

Not measurable

RESULTS

Interest satisfaction must be achieved if reform is to be accepted.

---

eryone's needs, but is not located on the A-B line. For example, imagine you have a limited amount of salary money available to disperse among faculty members. Rather than argue with a faculty member over your position of $3,000 and his or her position of $4,000, investigate whether the faculty member will settle for an extra $500 to $1,000 travel-expense allocation out of a more plentiful source of funds (point C).

3. *Criteria: Base resolution on objective standards.* Department chairs and faculty must find fair standards and procedures to achieve desired ends. Bring standards of fairness, efficiency, or merit into the discussion and you will be more likely to produce a wise and fair resolution. In position resolution, you will spend time and energy defending your position and attacking the other side. If you base your agreement on consistent standards, such as precedent, equal treatment, tradition, market value, moral codes, or professional ethics, you will be less vulnerable to attack. Both you and your faculty must yield to principle, not to pressure, and keep the focus on interests.

To summarize, the principled method, in contrast to position resolution, focuses on the basic interests of both you and your faculty, while searching for mutually satisfying options based on fair standards and procedures; this typically leads to wise outcomes or agreements (Table 6.4). Once you separate personalities from problems, you will be able to deal with faculty empathetically, as human beings in search of a satisfying resolution and an amicable agreement.

Traditionally, the positional resolution of conflict calls for taking sides, either through hard or soft negotiations. Chairs are typed as one face of Janus or the other—faculty or administration. Soft department chairs emphasize the importance of building and maintaining relationships; they approach conflict as friends, seeking agreement, making offers, and yielding to pressure. In contrast,

---

Exercise 6.3 Faculty Interest Inventory

The foundation of conflict resolution is the knowledge that you can articulate the interests of your faculty. On the right side of the matrix below, identify your faculty members. Across the top, write your perception of each faculty member's primary interest and secondary interest.

Remember, interests are intangible or abstract needs, such as values, principles, or motivations. They are rarely negotiable and not measurable.

FACULTY MEMBER	PRIMARY INTEREST	SECONDARY INTEREST
A.		
B.		
C.		
D.		
E.		
F.		
G.		

hard department chairs see faculty as adversaries who seek victory, make threats, and apply pressures.

You do not have to choose between hard or soft styles of resolution. The above principles empower you to change the rules of the game and approach conflict from a principled point of view. You can work with faculty as mutual problem-solvers, seeking wise outcomes by exploring interests and yielding to principle, not pressure. Table 6.5 displays the contrasting highlights of these three conflict resolution approaches.

THE CONFLICT RESOLUTION CONTINUUM

The preceding discussion on resolution may lead you to believe that your primary role in conflict is to negotiate an equitable settlement, protecting the interests of others and yourself at the same time. This assumes that you, personally, are in conflict with someone else: a student, faculty member, dean, or even another chair. Department chairs have a variety of means for resolving disputes. Table 6.6 illustrates some of these options, which vary in terms of formality of the process, privacy of the discussion, and the parties involved (Eunson 1997; Moore 1996).

On the left end of the continuum, at Level 1, the majority of disagreements are handled though private, informal discussion. On the far right of the continuum, at Level 5, lies the ground of litigation—the formal, regulated, public process involving third parties. In between these extremes (dialogic resolution and

---

Table 6.4 Principled Conflict Resolution Skills

I. Don't bargain
    • It endangers ongoing relationships.
    • It becomes difficult when more than two parties are involved.
    • It places all parties in a win/lose situation.

II. Separate the people from the problem
    • Recognize the individual.
    • Look for perceptions (actively listen, empathize).
    • Don't impute your feelings or concerns to others.
    • Avoid personal attacks.

III. Focus on interests
    • Behind each position lie both differing and compatible interests.
    • Identify interests (explore the why's and why not's).
    • Look forward—not back.
    • Be hard on the problem; be soft on the people.

IV. Invent options
    • Avoid premature judgments, examine your assumptions.
    • Be creative.
    • Look for mutual benefit (not win/lose).
    • Find additional resources and remove obstacles.

V. Use objective criteria
    • Find fair standards and fair procedures.
    • Establish common purpose, desired end results.
    • Yield to principle—not to pressure

Source: Fisher, R., and William Ury. 1983. *Getting to Yes.*

legal resolution) are three of the most commonly used techniques in conflict situations: negotiation, mediation, and arbitration.

Chairs will be able to deal more effectively with conflict if they know the key characteristics of these approaches and can take advantage of their strengths and weaknesses. For example, negotiation, mediation, and arbitration can be used separately or complementarily (see Fisher and Shapiro 2005; Ury 2007; Badaracco 1997). They are not mutually exclusive, and in some circumstances can be seen as sequential phases of a conflict resolution process.

Early phases of disagreement are primarily based on informal discussion, but if this proves inadequate, the dispute moves into negotiation, mediation, arbitration, and, ultimately, litigation. This is not to say that lower levels represent weaker strategies, but that other approaches are more appropriate under certain circumstances. As chair, most of your conflict occurs among faculty colleagues, so you should recognize your important role in assisting with the resolution of conflict among faculty. In addition to developing negotiation skills, you should understand the roles and skills required to mediate their conflicts.

Table 6.5 Ways to Resolve Conflict

SOFT	HARD	PRINCIPLED
Friends	Adversaries	Problem solver
Agreement	Victory	Wise outcome
Trust	Distrust	Independent of trust
Make offers	Make threats	Explore interests
Yield to pressure	Apply pressure	Yield to principle, not pressure

Source: Fisher, Roger, and William L. Ury. 1981. *Getting to Yes: Negotiating Agreement Without Giving In*. New York, NY: Penguin Books.

While the role of negotiator is often intuitively understood, mediation requires a different process, a different set of skills. As mediators, chairs need to perform the roles of conflict assessor, process convener, resource expander, reality tester, and active listener.

As developed by several dispute-resolution centers in the Western world, mediation follows a distinct procedure, and its process of resolution differs from that of the traditional negotiation session (Lincoln and O'Donnell 1986; Moses and Roe 1990). It is as much a science as an art. If you, as chair, accept the role of mediator, eight generic procedures should be used in the mediation process:

1. *Clarify the chair's role.* The mediator's main role is to get both sides to suggest solutions, not to make the final decision. Therefore, you need to be impartial and facilitate the presentation of facts, feelings, and proposals. You must use supportive, non-judgmental language and create a non-threatening environment where the disputants feel comfortable expressing themselves, their needs, and their aspirations. You must also see to it that the parties' understanding of each other's needs and interests facilitates a mutually acceptable solution.

2. *Invite opening statements from the disputants.* Have each of the disputants separately make opening statements as to their expectations for the mediation process. Reinforce that mediation is a voluntary process that can be terminated at any time.

3. *Develop presentation of issues and feelings.* As in a court of law, have the charging party go first and lay out the facts and feelings on their side of the case. The other side then shares their side of the story. Your responsibility is to actively listen and have the parties generate data.

Table 6.6 ConflictResolution Continuum

	CONFLICT RESOLUTION CONTINUUM				
	← Increase Use of Power and Less Control by Disputant →				
Levels	1. Discussion	2. Negotiation	3. Mediation	4. Arbitration	5. Litigation
KEY CHARACTERISTICS					
1. Formality	Informal/voluntary	Semi-formal/voluntary	Voluntary	Voluntary/required	Formal/required
2. Focus	Communicate positions/interests	Explore issues/interests	Explore issues/interests	Address questions, contested issues	Legal intervention on standards
3. Flexibility of procedures	Very high	Very high	Very high	Moderate	Low
4. Outcome	Develop promises	Decisions by disputants	Guided disputant decision	Arbitrator decision	Authoritative edict
ROLE OF DISPUTANTS					
5. Role of individuals	Air differences	Address issues/interests	Explore solutions	Submit evidence	Submit evidence thru attorney
6. Process	No formal procedures	Procedures open	Develop procedures	Procedures pre-established	Legal precedent/ develop procedures
7. Preservation of relationships	Very high	Very high	High	Doubtful	Very doubtful
8. Control of disputants	Very high	Very high	High	Moderate	Low
9. People involved	Discussants	Disputants	Use of mediator	Use of arbitrator	Imposition of advocates
NATURE OF SETTLEMENT					
10. Type of decision	Reduce tension	Resolve dispute	Mutual gain (win-win)	Right vs. wrong rectification	Conformity to case law/statutes
11. Amount of authority/coercion	Informal agreement	Mutual agreement	Mutual agreement	Arbitrator makes final & binding decision	Decision upheld by legal statutes

Source: Gmelch, W.H. 1998. The Janus Syndrome: Managing conflict from the middle. In S. Holton, ed., *Mending the Cracks in the Ivory Tower*.

4. *Clarify and elaborate the facts.* At this point you may ask for clarification of perceptions and verification of the facts as stated by each party. You may need to ask for more detail on specific issues and even have the parties repeat what was said as a means of sorting out errors in understanding. Through the use of summarization and paraphrasing, ensure appreciation and understanding of everyone's point of view.

5. *Help the parties move toward resolution.* Assess whether both parties are willing to begin resolving the conflict. In full session or by private caucus, ask for proposed remedies or points on which they agree, then help them isolate the issues that need to be resolved. You should realize that mediation may extend over a period of several sessions, with caucusing and perception-checking taking place between sessions.

6. *Solicit suggestions and contributions.* Have each party contribute equally to ideas for solutions that will satisfy everyone's needs. The more they develop their own ultimate solution, the more likely they will be to feel committed to upholding it.

7. *Reality-test solutions.* Once they have proposed solutions, ask how they will implement them. Based on what criteria? How would each suggested solution satisfy the other party's interests? Remember, interest satisfaction must be achieved if conflict is to be resolved.

8. *Summarize agreement and commitment.* It is your role to summarize what has been agreed and commit them to it, either in writing or by your witness as an objective third party. Each must leave with a clear picture of what has been achieved and what each party is obligated to do. While some conflicts may not be totally resolved, they may be better managed in the future.

Finally, congratulate both parties and reinforce anything they have found useful in resolving the current dispute. It is critical for the mediator to be neutral (Moses and Roe 1990). However, neutrality poses some problems if the parties have disproportionate power bases and abilities to articulate their cases. You must then assume a role in encouraging the less vocal faculty to speak up and express needs, for the minority opinions today may be the majority tomorrow.

INGREDIENTS FOR SATISFYING RESOLUTION

A durable resolution among faculty or between chairs and faculty must be achieved at three levels of settlement: substantive, procedural, and psychological (Lincoln and O'Donnell 1986). This point is paramount in preserving the civility and credibility of the expression of differences in the academy; we will elaborate it to underscore its importance. Regardless of the approach you use to resolve conflict in your department, whether it is mediation or negotiation, the key is its durability. In order to avoid a conflicted aftermath you must make sure that each party obtains all three levels of satisfaction.

Substantive satisfaction

While conflict-response styles speak to trading off substance against relationships, it is imperative that no matter what the trade-off, both parties feel a sense of adequate resolution. This can only be present if a reasonable level of interest-satisfaction is achieved. The key to substantive satisfaction is not ultimate resolution for one party over another, but an acceptable level of satisfaction for both.

Procedural satisfaction

The basic question is whether the parties were satisfied with the conflict proceedings before, during, and after the resolution. Who initiated the process? Where did the meetings take place—your office, a faculty member's office, or a neutral place, such as a conference room or the student union's cafeteria? The parties must feel they had control over the process and were not forced into any unusual, uncomfortable, or unfairly weighted procedures. The true test of procedural satisfaction is whether the parties would use the same process again.

Psychological satisfaction

As is the case with substantive satisfaction, a balance between relationships and substance must be achieved if parties are to be psychologically satisfied. If both parties feel better after resolution than before, psychological satisfaction has most likely occurred. Rather than feeling like a winner or loser, each disputant should have a sense of equity in the resolution and ownership in the solution.

A psychologically satisfying resolution will provide extra benefits to both parties and the department:

1. Compliance with the agreement will be more likely.

2. Sabotage of the settlement will probably not occur.

3. Renewal of the dispute is less likely.

4. Anxiety of both the chair and faculty is relieved.

5. Healthier communication patterns are established for earlier resolution next time.

6. Both faculty and administration feel better after settlement, which adds to the spirit of a departmental team (see chapter 2).

In the process of day-to-day interaction, all communities, universities, departments, and interpersonal relationships experience conflict at one time or another. The department environment, the diversity of faculty members, and the differences in chairs' preferred conflict resolution styles all limit the possibility of having collegial and civil academic colleagues who function as a team.

In conclusion, there is probably very little in this chapter that you do not already know intuitively. The purpose is to expose you to the issues surrounding conflict management and help you organize your conflict resolution approach into a creative, useable framework comprised of the three Rs of conflict: *recognition, response,* and *resolution.*

This is not a chapter on how to win in battle against faculty, but how to deal with interests such that you and your faculty find a satisfying resolution while enjoying mutual respect and maintaining positive and productive relationships. If you believe the principles discussed in this chapter will help you, share them with your adversaries. Unlike most other strategies, if the other side becomes equally skilled, it becomes easier, not more difficult, to reach agreement. The next step is yours.

Chapter 7

STRESS MANAGEMENT

Mending the Cracks in the Department

> What is urgent is seldom important
> and what is important is seldom urgent.
> — Dwight D. Eisenhower

For many academics, life consists of work. Over 60 percent of administrators have nothing of greater meaning in their lives than work—and since chairs work an average of fifty-six hours per week, over half of their waking hours are consumed by work. Work and the role of chair often define one's identity and self-concept, which in turn dictate who one socializes with, where one lives, how long one lives there, and what lifestyle one leads. Obviously, administration plays an important part in a chair's life and provides pleasures as well as pressures.

What is the price of venturing into administration? Where does it lead? What are the benefits? And what leadership challenges does it present for the future? The answers to these and other questions regarding the challenges of leadership are addressed in this chapter on stress management.

Many provosts and presidents contend that the most critical role in the university is that of the department chair. Deans add that their success depends on the leadership capabilities of department chairs. The position of department chair is one the most complex, elusive, and intriguing management positions in America. It is unique, not least because most department chairs are called upon to teach, conduct research, and keep up with their disciplines. What other management position requires the continuation of previous responsibilities while adding to them a whole new demanding role?

Despite the unique and important role chairs play in universities, few researchers have ventured to study this multidimensional position. While the recent literature is beginning to address the challenges of department chairs (see Gmelch and Miskin 2004; Gmelch and Schuh 2004; Hecht, Higgerson, Gmelch, and Tucker 1999; Lucas 2000; Wheeler, et al., 2008), most of the previous literature has been anecdotal. Based on several national and international studies, this chapter addresses the stress traps of the department chair. While it explicitly addresses department chairs, it is relevant to all academic administrators whose responsibilities involve mentoring, supporting, and working with department chairs, people who deal with stress as a constant in their everyday lives.

As mentioned in chapter 1, chairs typically begin their positions without leadership training, without a clear understanding of the time demands, without knowing the conflict inherent in the position, and without an awareness of the stress and demands on their academic careers and personal lives. Many chairs love to help students and serve their colleagues—that is why they *are* chairs—but return to faculty status after a single term of the frenzied, conflicting demands that all chairs encounter. What is known about this phenomenon called stress? And what can academics do to control stress and make the job of department chair more satisfying?

This chapter presents strategies for coping with stress. First, it explores the nature of stress and dispels the common myths that can impede stress control. Next, it presents a four-stage model of the stress cycle and a framework for managing stress. We will explore each stage of the stress cycle and identify techniques to master the stresses of chairing a department. Finally, we will place issues of stress in the context of 1) trade-offs in chairs' professional and personal lives and 2) the tension between scholarship and leadership.

COMMON MYTHS ABOUT STRESS

It will be useful to begin by addressing the most common misconceptions regarding stress.

Myth #1: Stress is harmful. While the popular perception is that stress is unpleasant or negative, it can be positive as well. The Chinese ideogram for stress contains two characters, one signaling danger, the other opportunity. Just so, stress actually encompasses both distress (bad or unpleasant events) and eustress (good or pleasant events). Over time, the old French and Middle English word "distress," with its negative connotation, blended with the English "stress." We would do well to remember that while failure is stressful, so is success.

Myth #2: Stress should be avoided. Stress is a natural part of life and helps individuals respond to threat or rise to challenge. It cannot and should not be avoided, for without stress we could not live. What "under stress" actually means is that someone is under *excessive* pressure or distress. An analogous condition is that of "running a temperature": body temperature itself is essential to life, and having a high temperature is one of the body's natural adaptive strategies. When handled properly, stress can be the spice of life.

Myth #3: The higher up in the organization, the greater the stress. It is popularly believed that high-level executives lead the list of heart-disease patients. However, a Metropolitan Life Insurance Company study challenged this assumption when it found that presidents and vice presidents of the five hundred largest industrial corporations suffered 40 percent fewer heart-attack deaths than middle managers of the same companies. Similar data support the conclusion that middle managers have a higher peptic ulcer rate than chief executive officers. Data about academe are mixed in terms of who suffers the most from stress. One study we conducted found that department chairs reported greater stress than all other classifications of faculty (resident instructional faculty, librarians, student services, and cooperative extension) as well as other academic administrators (Gmelch and Wilke 1991). In a comparative study of twenty-three occupations, professors in administrative posts ranked first, ahead of professors (who were sixth), in reported stresses and strains (Caplan et al. 1980). In addition, professors reported more satisfaction with their jobs than professors serving as administrators.

Myth #4: Stress is a predominantly male phenomenon. Until the 1980s, the literature commonly referred to "men under stress." While this misguided association with men no longer prevails, it is well known that men suffer higher rates of alcoholism, ulcers, lung cancer, suicide, and heart disease than women. However, over the past twenty years, as the number of women in predominantly male professions has increased, so has the incidences of stress and stress-related diseases among women. In a national study of professors' stress, we found that female faculty reported more stress than men, and married women experienced even more stress than single female professors (Gmelch, Lovrich, and Wilke 1984).

THE CHAIR STRESS CYCLE

Rather than avoiding stress, it is important for an administrator to control it and use it to advantage. The four-stage Chair Stress Cycle (Figure 7.1) offers an overview and explanation of the stress stages, and introduces a framework for action. The process begins with Stage I, *stressors*, a set of specific demands. Excessive meetings, interruptions, and confrontations are some common stressors. How much stress they produce depends on Stage II, the department chair's *perception* of them. If the person experiencing them does not have the physical or mental resources to meet the demands placed on him or her, the demand will be perceived as a stress trap. Stress created by this discrepancy between *demand* and *personal resources* results in a specific stress *response*—Stage III.

Figure 7.1 The Chair Stress Cycle

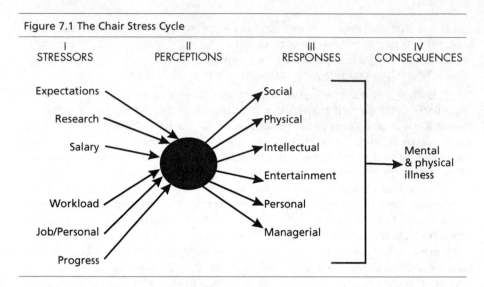

The fourth and final stage, *consequences*, pertains to the intensity and long-range negative effects of stress.

The stress cycle defines stress as: a person's anticipation of his or her inability to respond (Stage III) adequately to perceived (Stage II) demands (Stage I), accompanied by the anticipation of negative consequences (Stage IV) owing to inadequate responses. Note that this definition is couched in negative terms: inability, inadequate response, and negative consequences. However, your stress can be positive, stimulated by challenge or excitement. It's possible to transform a negative outcome into a positive one by changing perception of *inability* to perception of ability, i.e., the anticipation of the *ability* to respond adequately to a perceived demand, accompanied by the anticipation of a *positive* consequence following an *adequate* response.

This chapter focuses on the four stages of the stress cycle: identification of stressors in Stage I; investigation of susceptibility to stress in Stage II; broadening the repertoire of effective coping responses in Stage III; and converting the possible negative consequences in Stage IV from extreme anxiety and illness to mental equilibrium and even health, through a stress-absorption plan. If the stressors can be identified, negative perceptions turned into positive perceptions, and a variety of responses deployed in numerous ways, the department chair will enjoy a healthy and productive life.

STRESS TRAPS: STAGE I

Controlling the four-stage stress cycle begins with examining the demands of your current situation. The key to stress reduction is identifying your stress

TABLE 7.1 Ranking of Stressors

RANK	STRESS QUESTIONNAIRE ITEM	MEAN
1.	Having insufficient time to stay current in my academic field	3.9
2.	Trying to gain financial support for department programs	3.5
3.	Evaluating faculty and staff performance	3.4
4.	Attending meetings which take up too much time	3.3
5.	Feeling I have too heavy a workload	3.3
6.	Believing my academic career progress is not what it should be	3.3
7.	Writing letters and memos, and responding to other paperwork	3.2
8.	Imposing excessively high self-expectations	3.2
9.	Preparing manuscripts for publication	3.1
10.	Meeting report and other paperwork deadlines	3.1
11.	Making decisions that affect the lives of faculty, staff, and students	3.1
12.	Preparing budgets and allocating resources	3.0
13.	Seeking compatibility among institutional, departmental, and personal goals	3.0
14.	Securing financial support for my research	2.9
15.	Feeling required paperwork is not utilized	2.9
16.	Having inadequate time for teaching preparation	2.9
17.	Complying with college and university rules and regulations	2.8
18.	Participating in work-related activities outside regular hours	2.8
19.	Trying to influence the actions and decisions of my dean	2.7
20.	Receiving insufficient recognition for performing administrative responsibilities	2.7
21.	Handling student concerns and conflicts	2.7
22.	Supervising and coordinating the tasks of many people	2.6
23.	Receiving inadequate salary	2.6
24.	Having insufficient authority to perform my departmental responsibilities	2.4
25.	Resolving differences with my dean	2.3
26.	Trying to satisfy the concerns of constituent groups (alumni, community, etc.)	2.2
27.	Meeting social obligations (clubs, parties, volunteer work) expected of chairs	2.2
28.	Feeling others don't understand my goals and expectations	2.1
29.	Having a non-conducive work environment (e.g. crowded, noisy, inadequate facilities)	2.1
30.	Not knowing how my dean evaluates my performance	2.1
31.	Receiving insufficient recognition for research performance	2.1
32.	Feeling I will not be able to satisfy the conflicting demands of those in positions of authority over me	2.0
33.	Believing I can't get all of the information I need to carry out my job properly	2.0
34.	Making presentations at professional meetings	1.9
35.	Adapting to technological changes (e.g., fax, telephone systems, computers)	1.8
36.	Having to travel to fulfill job expectations	1.8
37.	Feeling I am not adequately trained to handle my job	1.7

TABLE 7.1 Ranking of Stressors con't

RANK	STRESS QUESTIONNAIRE ITEM	MEAN
38.	Believing my administrative career progress is not what it should be	1.7
39.	Feeling pressure for better job performance above what I feel is reasonable	1.6
40.	Feeling I have too much responsibility delegated to me by my dean	1.6
41.	Feeling not enough is expected of me by my dean	1.3

Note: Stress scale ranges from 5 (most stressful) to 1 (least stressful).

Source: Gmelch, Walter H., John S. Burns, et al. 1992. *Center for the Study of the Department Chair: 1992 Survey*. Pullman, WA: Washington State University.

traps. It may help to understand the more common stressors that beset department chairs and administrators.

Table 7.1 presents forty-one common causes of stress among department chairs, as derived from a series of national and institutional studies. To ensure that all potentially relevant facets of chair-related stress were identified, the items on the Chair Stress Inventory (CSI) were drawn from several sources. First, chairs kept stress logs for a period of two weeks in order to indicate on a daily basis the most stressful single event and the most stressful series of events. Second, a survey was conducted of chair job descriptions in search of additional stressors not already discovered by the stress logs. Third, other instruments developed to assess stress in academe were investigated for additional items. Finally, two studies of department chairs were conducted, one at a comprehensive university (Gmelch and Wilke 1991) and another in one hundred institutions of higher education (Gmelch and Burns 1993, 1994). The compilation of items from all four sources resulted in the forty-one item Chair Stress Inventory (see Exercise 7.1).

A factor analysis of these stressors discloses five sets of characteristics: administrative tasks, faculty role, role ambiguity, hierarchical authority, and perceived expectations (Gmelch and Miskin 1993). Below, the stressors are grouped according to which characteristics they embody:

1. Administrative-task stress

   - Meeting report and other paperwork deadlines
   - Preparing budgets and allocating resources
   - Trying to gain financial support for department programs
   - Writing letters and memos, and responding to other paperwork
   - Evaluating faculty and staff performance
   - Having to make decisions that affect the lives of faculty, staff, and students

- Feeling I have too heavy a workload
- Supervising and coordinating the tasks of many people
- Complying with college and university rules and regulations
- Attending meetings which take up too much time
- Handling student concerns and conflicts
- Seeking compatibility among institutional, departmental, and personal goals

2. Faculty-role stress

- Preparing manuscripts for publication
- Securing financial support for my research
- Believing my academic career progress is not what it should be
- Receiving insufficient recognition for research performance
- Having insufficient time to stay current in my academic field

3. Role-ambiguity stress

- Feeling I am not adequately trained to handle my job
- Feeling I have too much responsibility delegated to me by my dean
- Feeling not enough is expected of me by my dean
- Believing I can't get all the information I need to carry out my job
- Feeling others don't understand my goals and expectations
- Trying to satisfy the concerns of constituent groups (alumni, community, etc.)

4. Hierarchical authority stress

- Not knowing how my dean evaluates my performance
- Trying to influence the actions and decisions of my dean
- Receiving insufficient recognition for administrative responsibilities
- Having insufficient authority to perform my departmental responsibilities
- Feeling I will not be able to satisfy the conflicting demands of those in positions of authority over me
- Resolving differences with my dean
- Feeling pressure for better job performance above what I feel is reasonable

- Believing my administrative career progress is not what is should be
- Feeling required paperwork is not utilized
- Receiving inadequate salary

5. Perceived expectations stress

- Having to travel to fulfill job expectations
- Participating in work-related activities, outside regular working hours, that conflict with personal activities
- Meeting social obligations (clubs, parties, volunteer work) expected of chairs
- Making presentations at professional meetings
- Imposing excessively high self-expectations

(Source: Gmelch et al., 1992, Center for Academic Leadership, Washington State University.)

The *administrative tasks* category deals with three areas of managerial roles and responsibilities: administrative details in terms of meetings, workload, paperwork, deadlines, and budgets and financial support; personnel administration, including handling student conflicts, evaluating staff and faculty, supervising and coordinating personnel, and having to make decisions that affect the lives of faculty, staff, and students; and organizational constraints, highlighting the frustrations of complying with college and university regulations and seeking compatibility among institutional, departmental, and individual goals.

Department chairs seem to be caught between these administrative stresses and those of the regular *faculty role:* keeping current in their disciplines, preparing manuscripts, searching for money for their research, and making presentations. In addition, they feel that their academic career progress is not what it should be, possibly owing to serving as department chair. Thus, chairs are trapped between the pressures and demands of performing not only as administrators, but also as a productive faculty members.

From this Janus position emerges the *role ambiguity* factor. As indicated in Table 7.1, chairs basically experience stress due to the uncertainties and inadequacies of the chair position. These uncertainties reflect the typical research descriptions of role ambiguity. This recurring "academic administrator" theme (chair as faculty/chair as administrator) is visible when comparing the most serious stressors of chairs with those of faculty. Table 7.2 contrasts two national stress studies, one of chairs and the other of college faculty (Gmelch, Burns, Carroll, Harris, and Wentz 1992; Gmelch, Wilke, and Lovrich 1984).

Note first that not only do chairs identify seven of the professors' most serious stressors as their own, but the percent of chairs suffering from these stressors is higher in each case except for "excessively high self-expectations" (typi-

Table 7.2 Comparison of Stressors

STRESSORS	CHAIRS		PROFESSORS	
	Rank	Serious Stress	Rank	Serious Stress
Heavy workload	1	59%	5.5	40%
Obtaining program approval	2	54%	N/A	N/A
Keeping current	3	53%	3	49%
Complying with rules	4	48%	(Not ranked in top 13)	
Job interfering with personal time	5	47%	7	35%
Decisions affecting others	6	46%	(Not ranked in top 13)	
Excessive self-expectations	7	45%	1	53%
Resolving collegial differences	8	45%	(Not ranked in top 13)	
Evaluating faculty	9	42%	N/A	N/A
Completing paperwork	10	41%	(Not ranked in top 13)	
Preparing manuscripts	11	40%	5.5	40%
Telephone/visitor interruptions	12	40%	9.5	33%
Meetings	13	40%	9.5	33%

Source: Gmelch, Walter H., and John S. Burns. 1993. A National Study of Stress and Department Chairs. *Innovative Higher Education.*

cally more troublesome for faculty than administrators). This paradoxical situation of trying to fill a "swivel" position causes department chairs to feel double pressure to be an effective manager and productive faculty member.

Chairs' responsibility as representatives of the department to the dean and to higher administration is encompassed in the *hierarchical authority* stress factor. This category contains six stressors involving relationships with the dean and higher authorities. Additional frustrations from this area include the elements of inadequate recognition, rewards, and career progression.

Probably most problematic for department chairs is the fifth factor, *perceived expectations*, which reflects the commitments and obligations chairs perceive as necessary to fulfill the expectations of their positions, e.g., travel, social commitments, and volunteer work. The most notable and powerful stressor in this factor is self-imposed "excessively high self-expectations." In other words, it may not be the influence of an oppressive hierarchy or demanding dean that causes the greatest concern—it may instead be the self-generated stress of expecting to achieve more than can be delivered.

Use the Chair Stress Inventory (Exercise 7.1) to identify which factors affect you most powerfully. For comparison, Table 7.3 reveals the ten most serious stressors faced by department chairs, based on a national study of eight hundred department chairs.

THE PERCEPTION OF STRESS: STAGE II

While the demands surrounding the chair position cannot always be diminished, your perception of them, attitude toward them, and approach to them are under your control and are, ultimately, what determine whether these demands become stress traps. Feelings of anxiety are usually attributed to outside conditions, rather than internal attitudes. Professors and chairs alike typically place the blame on college or university administration, state or corporate funding, regents, or other demanding stakeholders. In actuality, much of the stress experienced by academics is self-imposed; accordingly, individual personalities play an important role in determining how stressful academic conditions are. Stressors, by themselves, are objective demands that only become stress traps when perceived, subjectively, to be troublesome. Perceptions (Stage II) are thus the key to whether stress is generated or alleviated. Consider the definition of stress proposed earlier and realize the role of perception in this process: one's anticipation (which can be real or imaginary) of one's inability (the degree to which one feels prepared) to respond adequately to a *perceived demand* (the critical element of whether stress exists or not), accompanied by one's anticipation (again, this anticipation can be real or imaginary) of negative consequences following an inadequate response.

It is how one approaches the job and life that causes most stress. Perception plays the major role in one's resilience to, or acceptance of, job stress. Although it is difficult to establish clear causal links between personality factors and disease, sufficient research evidence exists to document the link between certain types of behaviors and, at one extreme, heart disease, cancer, arthritis, asthma, as well as migraine headaches and the like. This evidence is too strong to dismiss and too critical to overlook.

Type A Department Chairs

Particularly deserving of attention is the Type A chair, who is prone to coronary heart disease (Friedman and Rosenman 1974). Since heart disease remains the number one killer in the United States, managing "Type A behavior" through perceptual awareness may save a life.

Exercise 7.1 Chair Stress Inventory

The following work-related situations have been identified as potential sources of stress. It is likely that some of these situations cause you more concern than others. Indicate to what extent each is a source of work-related stress by checking the appropriate response.

	LEVEL OF STRESS: Slight	Moderate			High
	1	2	3	4	5
1. Participating in work-related activities, outside regular working hours, that conflict with personal time	☐	☐	☐	☐	☐
2. Meeting social obligations (clubs, parties, volunteer work) expected of chairs	☐	☐	☐	☐	☐
3. Complying with college and university rules and regulations	☐	☐	☐	☐	☐
4. Having a non-conducive work environment (e.g. crowded, noisy, inadequate facilities)	☐	☐	☐	☐	☐
5. Making presentations at professional meetings	☐	☐	☐	☐	☐
6. Imposing excessively high self-expectations	☐	☐	☐	☐	☐
7. Handling student concerns and conflicts	☐	☐	☐	☐	☐
8. Resolving differences with my dean/supervisor	☐	☐	☐	☐	☐
9. Having insufficient time to stay current in my academic field	☐	☐	☐	☐	☐
10. Having insufficient authority to perform my departmental responsibilities	☐	☐	☐	☐	☐
11. Believing my administrative career progress is not what it should be	☐	☐	☐	☐	☐
12. Believing my academic career progress is not what it should be	☐	☐	☐	☐	☐
13. Having to travel to fulfill job expectations	☐	☐	☐	☐	☐
14. Securing financial support for my research	☐	☐	☐	☐	☐
15. Preparing manuscripts for publication	☐	☐	☐	☐	☐
16. Receiving insufficient recognition for performing administrative responsibilities	☐	☐	☐	☐	☐
17. Feeling required paperwork is not utilized	☐	☐	☐	☐	☐
18. Having inadequate time for teaching preparation	☐	☐	☐	☐	☐
19. Writing letters and memos, and responding to other paperwork	☐	☐	☐	☐	☐
20. Feeling I have too heavy a workload	☐	☐	☐	☐	☐
21. Attending meetings which take up too much time	☐	☐	☐	☐	☐
22. Trying to influence the actions and decisions of my dean/supervisor	☐	☐	☐	☐	☐

Exercise 7.1 Chair Stress Inventory con't

	LEVEL OF STRESS:	Slight 1	2	Moderate 3	4	High 5
24.	Seeking compatibility among institutional, departmental, and personal goals	□	□	□	□	□
25.	Receiving insufficient recognition for research performance	□	□	□	□	□
26.	Not knowing how my dean/supervisor evaluates my performance	□	□	□	□	□
27.	Receiving inadequate salary	□	□	□	□	□
28.	Evaluating faculty and staff performance	□	□	□	□	□
29.	Trying to satisfy the concerns of constituent groups (alumni, community, etc.)	□	□	□	□	□
30.	Supervising and coordinating the tasks of many people	□	□	□	□	□
31.	Feeling others don't understand my goals and expectations	□	□	□	□	□
32.	Feeling I am not adequately trained to handle my job	□	□	□	□	□
33.	Believing I can't get all of the information I need to carry out my job properly	□	□	□	□	□
34.	Feeling I will not be able to satisfy the conflicting demands of those in positions of authority over me	□	□	□	□	□
35.	Feeling not enough is expected of me by my dean/supervisor	□	□	□	□	□
36.	Feeling pressure for better job performance above what I feel is reasonable	□	□	□	□	□
37.	Having to make decisions that affect the lives of faculty, staff, and students	□	□	□	□	□
38.	Feeling I have too much responsibility delegated to me by my dean/supervisor	□	□	□	□	□
39.	Meeting report and other paperwork deadlines	□	□	□	□	□
40.	Preparing budgets and allocating resources	□	□	□	□	□
41.	Trying to gain financial support for departmental programs	□	□	□	□	□

	Slight 1	2	Moderate 3	4	High 5
Assess the overall level of stress you experience as a chair	□	□	□	□	□
What percentage of the total stress in your life results from being a department chair?		____%			

Table 7.3 Top Department Chair Stressors

1. Insufficient time to keep current in academic field
2. Gaining financial support for department programs
3. Evaluating faculty and staff performance
4. Attending meetings which take up too much time
5. Feeling I have too heavy a workload
6. Believing my academic career progress is not what it should be
7. Writing letters, memos, and responding to other paperwork
8. Imposing excessively high self-expectations
9. Preparing manuscripts for publication
10. Meeting report and other paperwork deadlines

Source: Gmelch et al. 1992. Center for Academic Leadership, Washington State University.

Type As approach their jobs with intensity and impatience, so much so that they are attacked by heart disease at triple the rate of more relaxed and easygoing Type Bs. But what exactly is Type A behavior, and to what extent do department chairs exhibit it? A Type A chair can be characterized as an overly competitive achiever, aggressive, a fast worker, impatient, restless, hyperalert, explosive in speech, tense, and always feeling under pressure. Type B behavior is the polar opposite: relaxed, easygoing, seldom impatient, taking more time to enjoy things in life besides work, not easily irritated, works steadily, seldom lacks time, not preoccupied with social achievement, moving and speaking more slowly.

But who are the Type As? Are they more prevalent among chairs than faculty? Are you Type A? A major study entitled *Job Demands and Worker Health* investigated the prevalence of Type A personality characteristics in twenty-three occupations, including professors and academic administrators (Caplan et al. 1980). First the bad news: two occupations had by far the highest scores on the Type A index: academic administrators and family physicians. Table 7.4 shows that academic administrators (e.g., department chairs and directors) ranked first in Type A behavior, while professors ranked sixth. Note that the professors' scores were one third lower on the index than those of academic administrators. In addition, 12 percent of the academic administrators in this study suffered from coronary heart disease—three times the proportion of professors.

What might be some of the contributors to this higher incidence of heart disease and Type A behavior? Could it be the overtime administrators put into their jobs? Not at first glance. Table 7.4 shows that professors and academic administrators report working twelve and sixteen hours, respectively, beyond the traditional forty-hour week. Nevertheless, professors report only 31 percent

Table 7.4 Influences on Occupational Stress

OCCUPATION	1 TYPE A	2 % CORONARY HEART DISEASE	3 HOURS WORKED PER WEEK	4 OVERTIME PER WEEK
Administrative Professor	155	12.0	56.4	11.4
Physician	149	12.5	58.4	6.7
Tool & Die Worker	123	14.3	46.9	4.3
Administrator	111	8.3	48.7	6.4
Supervisor/Blue Collar	108	4.8	47.6	6.8
Scientist	106	5.1	46.6	5.0
Professor	106	4.1	51.6	3.6
Air Traffic Controller	102	3.7	38.1	0.4
Train Dispatcher	98	9.3	41.7	2.8
Supervisor/White Collar	5	4.8	43.7	3.8
Air Traffic Controller (small airport)	94	0.0	38.7	0.9
Electronic Technician	93	9.7	40.2	2.2
Police Officer	89	2.7	46.1	6.4
Forklift Driver	87	10.9	40.4	3.5
Courier	85	5.0	39.1	1.7
Assembly Worker	84	5.8	41.9	5.7
Engineer	82	5.5	43.3	3.6
Machine Tender	81	5.9	42.9	4.3
Accountant	74	12.0	40.6	1.9
Assembler/Relief	74	3.7	40.5	3.0

(3.6 hours) of their 12 hours as overtime that they didn't want to work, whereas academic administrators report 70 percent (11.4 hours) of their overtime as unwanted. In other words, the extra hours beyond the forty-hour work week are seen in a more positive light by professors and in a less positive light by administrators. As the study points out, many professors see the hours beyond a forty-hour week not as overtime, but simply as part of the time they need to perform their duties as they desire: "I would work the hours anyway, even if no one asked me," commented one professor, summing up this viewpoint. The administrative professor, however, views those extra hours as busywork (Caplan et al. 1980, 124). All in all, academic administrators put in more unwanted overtime than anyone else (professors are about average).

However, here's the good news for chairs: studies also show that, compared to the other twenty-two professions, academic administrators ranked second in personal flexibility; they ranked first in participation with others in decisions, as well as in social support from others at work, from spouses, from friends, and from relatives. Chairs were also highest in job fit and lowest in job boredom. They seem to have built in some resistance to stress attacks, and can never be accused of being bored!

Are You Type A?

But you are still wondering if you are Type A, right? Answer the questions in Exercise 7.2 to see. Better yet, ask your spouse, secretary, or closest colleague to answer the questions for you. Assessing your own personality seldom yields accuracy; true Type A's will deny having these traits.

As you probably concluded from the exercise, few individuals fall purely into either extreme. If you have classified yourself as an A, do not let this alone cause you to return to the less-Type-A faculty status. There are many techniques available to assist you in becoming shades of Type B, if you choose.

Coping with Type A behavior

Since coping is an individual art, some of the following techniques will work for you and others will not. Test them and others until you develop your own approach to a more positive perceptual focus (Stage II).

1. *Plan some personal time each day.* Don't operate from a crisis position. Schedule your day to encourage a more positive attitude. Plan a little idleness into each day. Each morning, arrive at the office a little early to set the stage for the day before the onslaught of interruptions, demands, and conflicts. At noon, make sure you take a mid-day break and have lunch with a colleague or engage in vigorous exercise to cut the eight-to-five stress cycle. Although this may sound counterintuitive, leave the office half an hour late in the evening in order to plan the next day and possibly avoid rush-hour traffic.

Exercise 7.2 Type Your Behavior

Answer the following questions by indicating what most often applies to you:

Yes   No

___ ___ 1. Do you feel compelled to do most things in a hurry?

___ ___ 2. Are you usually the first one through during a meal?

___ ___ 3. Is it difficult for you to relax, even for a few hours?

___ ___ 4. Do you hate to wait in line at a restaurant, bank, or store?

___ ___ 5. Do you frequently try to do several things at the same time?

___ ___ 6. Are you generally dissatisfied with what you have accomplished in life?

___ ___ 7. Do you enjoy competition and feel you always have to win?

___ ___ 8. When other people speak slowly, do you find yourself trying to rush them along by finishing the sentence for them?

___ ___ 9. Do you become impatient when someone does the job slowly?

___ ___ 10. When engaged in conversation, do you usually feel compelled to tell others about your own interests?

___ ___ 11. Do you become irritated when something is not done exactly right?

___ ___ 12. Do you rush through your tasks to get them done as quickly as possible?

___ ___ 13. Do you feel you are constantly under pressure to get more done?

___ ___ 14. In the past few years, have you taken less than your allotted vacation time?

___ ___ 15. While listening to other people, do you usually find your mind wandering to other tasks and subjects?

___ ___ 16. When you meet aggressive people, do you usually feel compelled to compete with them?

___ ___ 17. Do you tend to talk fast?

___ ___ 18. Are you too busy with your job to have time for hobbies and outside activities?

___ ___ 19. Do you seek and need recognition from your boss and peers?

___ ___ 20. Do you take pride in working best "under pressure"?

	A1		A2		B1		B2		
20 18	16	14	12	10	8	6	4	2	0

Number of "Yes" answers

Source: Gmelch, Walter H. 1982. *Beyond Stress to Effective Management.*

2. *Compartmentalize chair and non-chair activities.* One of the most difficult tasks for chairs to perform is separating administrative and scholarly activities. It may be helpful to compartmentalize, or separate, your administrative and academic duties. Similarly, you should separate work (professional) from non-work (personal) activities in order to have higher-quality, guilt-free evenings and weekends.

3. *Do one task at a time.* A typical Type A chair eats, walks, works, and talks all at the same time, engaging in what has been termed "polyphasic behavior"—that is, doing two or more things simultaneously. You can effectively only do one thing at a time, so select the most important task, whether it be administrative, academic, or personal, and do it first.

4. *Strive to enrich yourself: physically, socially, mentally, and emotionally.* A survey of four thousand executives found that less than 40 percent have any meaningful activity outside of work. Changing your perceptual focus requires activity and interest in more than one single area. Therefore, you need to take a holistic approach to personal enrichment through selected combinations of physical exercise, social interaction, mental stimulation, and emotional stability.

5. *Have a retreat away from the office.* Every chair should have some place where he or she can be alone. You need to be able to get away, close the door, and think without interruption—without faculty and staff making demands on your time and attention.

6. *Live by your calendar, not your watch.* Of the stressors faced by chairs, none is as pervasive as time. Break into your fragmented administrative life by setting time aside daily for organizing and planning. Rather than rushing around by the minute-hand of your watch, let your weekly calendar dictate your pace.

The stress of being a department chair is what you make of it. That can be the difference between coping and collapsing. The secret of success is not avoiding stressors in Stage I, but challenging them with a more positive perceptual response in Stage II. Whether you are exhausted or relaxed, under constant pressure or well paced, depends on how you approach the stress of crisis. Your personality, outlook, and perception can all work to either resist or intensify your stress. Are you thriving in your position, or is your personality killing you? Only you can tell.

The Coping Response: Stage III

While the literature on coping is significant in volume and diverse in attention, no one has been able to identify the perfect way to cope. Researchers from the disciplines of medicine, psychiatry, clinical psychology, behavioral science, and education have undertaken studies to understand the phenomenon of stress and coping responses.

The foremost authority on stress, Hans Selye, pointed out that despite everything that has been written and said about stress and coping, there is no ready-made formula that will suit everyone (1974). Since no one technique will suit everyone, how can department chairs positively respond to the stress traps identified in Stage I of the stress cycle? Blueprints for exact techniques are not available to chairs. Coping is an art, not a science.

Some researchers have attempted to define what constitutes effective and ineffective techniques for coping; for the most part, their results have been misleading. Others have proposed solutions based on such single techniques as relaxation, aerobics, and biofeedback. When developing a coping strategy, consider the following propositions as a base.

1. The individual is the most important variable. No single coping technique is effective for all department chairs in all colleges and universities. Therefore, coping techniques must be sensitive to each individual's character, as well as his or her cultural, social, psychological, and environmental circumstances.

2. Individuals can't change the world around them, and chairs can't change all the pressures they encounter in higher education; but they can change how they relate to them.

3. Individuals who cope best develop a repertoire of techniques to counteract different stressors in different situations. Using a repertoire of techniques constitutes an effective and a holistic approach to coping.

How chairs cope with stress

Are there identifiable categories of coping that, if used holistically, can help department chairs systematically address the stress of academic administration? To answer this question, we asked eight hundred department chairs, "Recognizing that being a chair is demanding, what have you found useful in handling the pressures of your job?" The majority of chairs cited more than one strategy. In all, they identified over eight hundred and eighty-seven coping responses. Content analysis of these responses revealed coping techniques grouped into seven categories. Rather than prescribing specific techniques, we suggest that you review the following categories to see which strategies are part of your repertoire.

1. Social support
   - having lunch with colleagues
   - talking it out with a trusted friend
   - sharing frustrations with spouse
   - complaining to other chairs about similar problems
   - consulting with the dean
   - developing companionship with friends outside the department
   - chatting informally with faculty at coffee breaks
   - developing a good working relationship with faculty, staff, and students
   - sharing problems with former chairpersons
   - confiding in the office staff
   - relying on the advice of selected colleagues
   - having a couple of confidants
   - participating in community activities
   - mentoring students and colleagues
   - spending leisure time with family
   - talking to myself a lot

2. Physical activities (Many universities and colleges resemble resorts, with all the sports and physical-exercise facilities a person could envision in a fancy getaway. Take advantage of them.)
   - jogging
   - swimming
   - walking
   - hiking
   - horseback riding
   - martial arts
   - skiing
   - sailing
   - tennis
   - racquetball
   - basketball
   - regular, structured physical workouts

3. Intellectual stimulation

- attending professional conferences
- reading biographies of political and military personalities
- the satisfaction of writing manuscripts
- staying active in research and setting aside time to concentrate on it ("at least one day a week, for without it I would go crazy")
- getting out of the office for field work or going to the library
- teaching at least once a year
- enjoying cultural events such as plays and art exhibits

4. Entertainment

- watching television
- going to a movie or out to dinner
- getting out of town
- taking a vacation, mini vacations, or weekend vacation
- listening to classical music
- reading novels
- attending concerts, art events, and such

5. Personal interests

- playing a musical instrument
- gardening
- gourmet cooking
- taking nature hikes
- working on arts or crafts
- creative writing
- taking a vocational classes
- other personal hobbies unrelated to work (some cited just plain "dropping out of sight")

6. Self-management

- delegating authority to faculty and staff
- using committees to share the workload
- involving faculty in decisions
- planning strategically
- being assertive and saying no
- being fair, open, and honest
- listening more than talking

- scheduling time off for self
- retreating to one's lab or private office
- setting goals (never making "department chair" the final goal in one's career!)
- being realistic about goals
- prioritizing work that focuses on goals
- clearing the desk every day
- effectively and efficiently using time
- building trust with colleagues
- hiring competent staff
- asking for help from department members
- reserving uninterrupted blocks of time for family and research
- keeping separate the life as a researcher and as a chair
- hibernating to work on activities requiring intense concentration
- partying whenever possible, or having a quiet social life
- dealing with conflict constructively
- having an excellent, dedicated secretary and administrative staff

7. Supportive attitudes

- being optimistic and keeping a positive outlook
- developing a sense of humor
- going home guilt-free ("even if it means late!")
- emotionally distancing oneself from the job ("leave the worry at the workplace—nothing goes home except me!")
- not taking on others' anxieties
- depersonalizing issues
- being patient
- minimizing self-importance
- knowing one's limitations
- laughing
- crying
- recognizing that some stress is normal

While no one of the responses taken separately presents *the* answer to coping, taken collectively, chairs can view these methods as comprising a coping taxonomy from which to seek their own stress reduction.

Coping with stress is a holistic proposition. It is much like weight loss: if one were to exercise more, but eat more too, the results might not be as beneficial as exercising more while cutting back or stabilizing one's diet. In much the same way, effective coping consists of building a repertoire of techniques equally balanced in the social, physical, intellectual, entertainment, managerial, personal, and attitudinal categories. Your goal is to reduce your stress by adding some of these techniques to your present repertoire of stress responses. It is not the chair who masters one technique that copes most effectively and creatively, but the one who possesses the flexibility to call upon any number of techniques from various sources—physical activity, managerial skills, social support, and so on.

FROM ILLNESS TO WELLNESS—CONSEQUENCES: STAGE IV

Behind the achievements of many great academics lies the factor of stress. Based on a study of 1,200 faculty members, Figure 7.2 shows how stress can interact with productivity (Wilke, Gmelch, and Lovrich 1985). A moderate amount of stress helped them reach peak performance; however, when stress reached "excessive" proportions (burnout), their performance significantly declined. Note also that without sufficient stress (lack of motivation or challenge—rustout), their performance also declined.

Department chairs often experience excessive stress. After all, they can only put out so many brush fires before eventually burning out themselves. It is at this point that stress becomes a most powerful and elusive enemy, playing a major role in a variety of illnesses. With proper management of the stress cycle, the end result of stress will be not illness, but wellness. Your stress cycle can be a positive, upward spiral toward mental and physical well being if you are able to manage your Stage I stressors, reinforce your resilience in Stage II, and develop a repertoire of positive coping techniques in Stage III. Doing so will help overcome the sense of being overwhelmed. To achieve complete equilibrium and a full sense of health requires going beyond stress management to adaptive, holistic stress-reduction practices.

DEPARTMENT CHAIR ACTION PLAN

The following action plan suggests dividing stressors into two categories: those within your control and those without. Those within your control should be managed at the cause level by self-management techniques. Those beyond your control should be attacked at the symptom level with stress absorbers such as relaxation, nutrition, exercise, and coping attitudes.

Figure 7.2 Stress and Performance

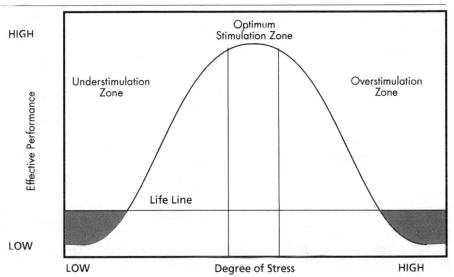

The majority of top stressors identified in the research relate directly to time, administrative tasks, academic endeavors, and personal expectations. Clearly, some of these stressors are more controllable than others. Most chairs would agree that they could, feasibly, become better managers of their time and personal expectations; on the other hand, it is more difficult to change salaries and other organizational constraints in tough economic and administrative climates.

Therefore, the key to stress reduction rests in a wise old adage: we should seek "the courage to change the things we can, the serenity to accept those we cannot, and the wisdom to know the difference." In other words, you need to identify which causes of stress are under your control, and resolve them. When it comes to those that are inherent in your job and cannot be controlled, you must learn to live with them, absorbing the pressure and attacking the symptoms rather than the causes.

The following action plan will help you successfully reduce those menacing stressors that are under your control. The purpose of the plan is to systematically dissect and redirect stressors by analyzing the *causes* of each, examining potential *solutions*, and finally taking corrective *actions*. Specifically, the steps of the plan are:

1. Identify a bothersome *stressor* over which you have some control.

2. Search for the *causes* of the stressful event.

3. Generate a set of possible *solutions* to remedy the causes.

Sample Action Plan

I. MOST BOTHERSOME STRESS EVENT:		
II. CAUSES	III. SOLUTIONS	IV. SPECIFIC ACTION PLAN
1.	1.	A. The plan is to:
2.	2.	
3.	3.	
4.	4.	

V. STEPS FOR IMPLEMENTATION	
1. Activity:	3. How often:
2. Where:	4. When:

VI. FOLLOW-UP EVALUATION	
1.	3.
2.	4.

VII. NEGATIVE UNINTENDED CONSEQUENCES	
1.	3.
2.	4.

© Gmelch, Walter H. Center for Academic Leadership, University of San Francisco.

4. Specify a *plan* to alleviate the causes.

5. Develop a *timetable* to implement the plan.

6. Set a date and method of *follow-up* and evaluate the effectiveness of the plan.

7. Investigate potential problems or *unintended consequences* the plan may have created.

While the Chair Action Plan may be seen as too mechanical and systematic, its logic is exactly what makes it work. An example is shown in Figure 7.3 of a completed worksheet examining the problem of "too heavy a workload." Eliminating the cause is the only way to truly alleviate stress.

For those stressors beyond your control, three other steps are needed to absorb the pressure: exercise, proper nutrition, and relaxation. These will provide you with a sound body and mind with which to cope with the onslaught of daily tensions and frustrations. Together with the holistic techniques in Stage III, you can have a full range of stress-reduction techniques, from managing to making, from solving the problems to absorbing the symptoms.

TRADE-OFFS: BALANCING TIME AND STRESS

Your ability to manage stress depends on how well you make trade-offs between professional and personal demands. Have you been able to keep a balance among your academic, leadership, and personal roles? Or do you perceive that you have accepted the leadership challenge at the expense of your professorial pleasures and personal enjoyments? This section addresses the stress trade-offs and concludes by highlighting the positive side of being a department chair (payoffs); it also suggests some balancing strategies for reducing stress.

1. Trade-offs act much like a ledger: a chair cannot debit one side without crediting the other. As professors assume the chair position, the credits added to the administrative side of the ledger must be debited against certain faculty activities. In other words, the chair position comes at some cost to faculty time, since time resembles a "zero-sum" game—everyone has twenty-four hours in a day, no less and no more.

   Hundreds of department chairs were asked whether they had spent more, the same, or less time in professional and personal activities since they became chairs. The results revealed a dramatic shift away from time devoted to research and writing, keeping current in the discipline, and teaching. Chairs reported spending 88 percent, 82 percent, and 56 percent less time in these activities, respectively. What has been your shift in professional time? Has it caused you concern and stress?

Figure 7.3 Action Plan — "Heavy Workload"

I. MOST BOTHERSOME STRESS EVENT: Too heavy a work load, one that cannot be finished in a day		
II. CAUSES	**III. SOLUTIONS**	**IV. SPECIFIC ACTION PLAN**
1. Unrealistic appraisal of time	1. Conduct time schedules	A. The plan is to: Concentrate on high-payoff tasks
2. Inability to say "no"	2. Gain assertive skills	B. Type of action
3. Overcommitted to family	3. Set family/job goals	_X_ corrective ___ interim
4. Unclear delineation of responsibilities	4. Request clear goals and outcomes	___ adaptive ___ preventive
5. Cannot distinguish between high and low priorities	5. Concentrate on high priorities	___ contingent

V. STEPS FOR IMPLEMENTATION

1. Activity: Develop "high-payoff and "low-payoff" lists	3. How often: Daily for two weeks
2. Where: In the office, at my desk, with no interruptions	4. When: Every morning at 8:30

VI. FOLLOW-UP EVALUATION

1. Did I write out my lists every morning?	3. Did I actually delegate or eliminate any low-payoff tasks?
2. Were the high-payoff tasks completed first?	4.

VII. NEGATIVE UNINTENDED CONSEQUENCES

1. My dean became upset with incomplete tasks important to him/her	3. I created an overload for my staff by delegating too many tasks to them
2. Work became too regimented and not as carefree	4.

MODIFICATIONS OF PLAN NEEDED? Since my dean needs to know what I am concentrating on (high-payoffs), I should communicate with him/her periodically to seek concurrence with my plan.

2. Trade-offs between professional and personal interests vie for the same resource—time. An almost equally pronounced percentage of chairs reduced their personal time with family (65 percent), friends (56 percent), and leisure (77 percent) due to administrative duties. Spiritual and civic activities, interestingly enough, remained "the same" for most chairs. Have you had less time for your family, friends, and leisure activities since assuming your chair responsibilities?

3. Trade-offs can create dissatisfaction with personal and professional lives. Chairs were asked if they were satisfied with the shifts in the way they allocated time as they entered administration. An overwhelming percent expressed dissatisfaction with debiting the time spent in scholarly writing and research (87.5 percent), in keeping current in the discipline (94 percent), in being with family (89 percent), in being with friends (87.5 percent), and in leisure (79.5 percent). As an aside, over 80 percent of the chairs believed that "their loads should be lightened to make more time for research, writing, or other work in the field," and that "if no opportunity were available to do personal research, [they] would find the job less satisfying." Ironically, those chairs who spent less time teaching were split: 55 percent satisfied and 45 percent dissatisfied with their reduced teaching loads. Are you dissatisfied with the shifts that have occurred in your time allocations?

4. Too many trade-offs in one direction create an imbalance and lead to negative stress. Is your position as chair a major contributor to the stress in your life? What percentage of the total stress in your life comes from being a chair? When this question was asked of 1,600 department chairs across the United States (Center for the Study of the Department Chair 1990, 1992), they perceived that 70 percent of the stress in their lives came from their job. Chairs seem to be trapped between the pressures and demands of performing not only as administrators, but also as productive faculty members. The academic versus administrator role-dilemma is a common song of despair among chairs, and is reinforced when chairs' most serious stressors are compared with those of faculty. For example, almost 60 percent of the chairs suffered from "heavy workloads," compared to 40 percent of the professors. Overall, chairs experience more stress than faculty. Not only do they seem to retain many of the highest faculty stressors while holding the chair position, they also add such managerial stressors as confrontation with colleagues, new time demands, and institutional constraints (Gmelch and Burns 1993).

5. Routine trade-off decisions usually favor the urgent over the important. Daily pressures and stresses usually result in the tyranny of the urgent, even though the most urgent tasks may not include the primary responsibilities of your job. Urgency is easily confused with priority, and urgent tasks can relegate true priorities to secondary status. For example, email responses may at times appear more pressing than faculty issues. If drafting a memo to the graduate school is really important, perhaps a quick telephone call instead of the memo could stave off the emergency, save an appointment with a faculty member, and keep you in balance.

   In the same spirit, many relatively unimportant tasks creep into your personal time unless you protect your calendar. Just as you take your professional calendar home and announce time commitments to your family and friends, you should also take your personal calendar to work and protect your personal commitments. For example, season tickets to plays, performances, and sports events should be written on your work calendar so you can protect their times and dates.

6. The clearer the distinction between personal and professional goals —and between academic and administrative goals—the less the potential conflict between their trade-offs. While we have focused primarily on resolving the 70 percent of stress generated by administrative factors, you should not ignore the other 30 percent created by non-job-related pressures, for two important reasons: First, your effectiveness as chair depends to a large extent on your ability to handle pressures from your private life. Second, managers need to approach their lifestyles holistically, trading off effectively between their personal and professional goals. In other words, in order to be an effective leader, you need to be an effective person altogether —parent, spouse, public servant, colleague, and professional. One cannot be unhealthy or ineffective in one's private life and still be an effective manager in one's professional life. In order to succeed, you must find the balance between your private and professional needs.

7. Trade-off decisions continue to favor one side or the other unless goals are established and updated periodically. Without personal goals or objectives to guide trade-off decisions, one side of the scale can engulf your energy and time. Lay out your goals for the semester, year, or term of office, rather than itemizing activities on a daily basis. Remember: without balance, you may return to faculty status and find that you are sorely outdated in your discipline, or you may reach the end of your professional career to find yourself out of touch with your important personal interests.

In order to prevent the imbalance caused by time, stress, and job dissatisfaction, chairs need to perform a number of these balancing acts and create a leadership position that both challenges and satisfies them as scholars serving as academic leaders.

BALANCING STRATEGIES

The purpose of this chapter has been to provide helpful suggestions for department chairs and administrators in their struggle to get personal stress under control. Excessive stress is a disease endemic to higher education, invading all aspects of the university: when it is left unchecked and undirected, psychological, emotional, and physical maladies hamstring department chairs, their work units, and the university itself. Listed below are a few final structural and personal ideas to make your position less stressful and more enjoyable.

Restructure the position

Work with your dean to reduce the expectations of the position to those befitting a half-time assignment. Negotiate proper support to manage the key responsibilities of the position. Besides office support, request a research assistant for the office-management team to conduct necessary reports for the university, state agencies, and outside constituencies.

Purge unnecessary administrivia

Related to restructuring the position is the need to reduce the amount of paperwork and requests for reports rarely read. Since the highest stress on chairs comes from overload, concentrate on your department's high-payoff activities, rather than those that are urgent but sometimes not so important. Each request should be measured against its contribution to the department's mission and goals.

Reverse the hierarchy

Traditionally and structurally, universities are top-down hierarchies. Chairs serve at the pleasure of, and in the service of, the dean and faculty. You might ask why deans exist. In part, the answer is to provide support and leadership for department chairs. Be proactive and seek your dean's help. In turn, you as chair should serve your faculty, just as everyone on the faculty serves the students.

Manage your management time

Paperwork, meetings, deadlines, and workload represent not the ends of managerial and academic productivity, but the means to important goals.

1. Identify high-payoff (HIPO, i.e., most important, rather than most urgent) activities that will contribute to excellence in both manage-

ment and faculty responsibilities. For example, budget, personnel, and personal-productivity activities should take precedence over administrative details, unimportant meetings, filing unread reports, and answering meaningless correspondence.

2. Reduce the involvement of chairs in less meaningful, low-payoff (LOPO) processes. This is the corollary of the first principle. You can find more time for HIPOs if you delegate or eliminate your LOPOs. The key for chairs is to identify the LOPOs so they can be ignored—a difficult task for most managers, since everything they do seems so important.

3. Develop a more efficient working environment so that: routine paperwork can be handled by office assistants, telephone calls can be screened, time can be blocked into uninterruptible periods for productive, thoughtful work, and, when possible, a HIPO hideout can be used as a retreat to prepare manuscripts and keep up with the academic discipline.

Confront conflict with integrity

As noted in chapter 6, the chairperson's most frequent and serious conflict arises in confronting peers, and on occasion, the dean. A few reminders may be helpful in working with your colleagues and the dean:

1. The power of the chair does not rest as much in the position (power of reward and punishment) as it does in the person (influence by personal credibility, expertise, and collegiality). Therefore, use the power of your position sparingly, and build a solid base of personal power with your dean and faculty by working with them in an open, honest, and professional manner.

2. When caught between the demands of administration and the needs of faculty, explore common interests that transcend and satisfy both parties.

3. Work on getting faculty involved and having them buy into the solutions—your role is more to facilitate than to direct.

Protect your scholarship interests

Data from our studies confirm that chairs need more time for their scholarly pursuits and personal interests while serving departments. If your time for keeping current in your discipline and research is not protected, you may become dissatisfied and more reluctant to continue as chair. Chairs' number one stressor is trying to keep current in the discipline. In addition, preparing manuscripts for publication and maintaining academic career progress also rank in the top ten chair stress traps. In essence, department chairs have become role prisoners of both faculty productivity pressures and administrative leadership challenges. If you find yourself falling into this pattern, protect your time and resources using an Academic Protection Plan:

1. Block uninterrupted periods of time to engage in thoughtful scholarly activities.

2. Maintain another office on campus or at home to ensure that the equivalent of a half-to-a-full day each week can be devoted to your academic endeavors.

3. Establish a research or writing team of faculty members and/or graduate students.

4. Negotiate a sabbatical between terms or at the end of the term to regain currency in the discipline.

Any approach to reducing chair stress rests both with the chair's willingness to seek creative solutions and the institution's responsiveness in developing effective and productive leadership. While the future of academic leadership may appear rife with stress, it is also replete with challenges and creative opportunities. Stress can be the spice of your life, if you handle it right!

Chapter 8

LEADERSHIP LEGACY, PAYOFFS, AND DEVELOPMENT

> Clearly then, we cannot do away with specialization,
> nor would we wish to. But in the modern world it has extended
> far beyond anything we knew in the past. . . . There are many tasks
> that can be effectively performed only by men and women
> who have retained some capacity to function as generalists—
> leadership and management. . . .
> — John W. Gardner

Your ability to develop a holistic managerial lifestyle depends on how well you make trade-offs between your professional and personal time and interests.

A personal or professional trade-off is defined as *an exchange of one interest in return for another; especially, a giving up of something desirable* (Greiff and Munther 1980). In essence, life is a trade-off, yet success depends in large measure on making effective trade-offs. In the case of being a department chair, have you been able to keep a balance among your academic, administrative, and personal roles? Or do you perceive that you have accepted the leadership challenge at the expense of your personal and professorial pleasures?

Taking the position of department chair raises four central questions that will impact the degree to which your trade-offs are effective: 1) Have you been able to continue professional and personal activities you enjoyed before becoming chair? 2) If your time has shifted significantly among faculty, managerial, and personal activities, are you satisfied with these changes? 3) What stresses and pressures were created when you assumed the chair position? 4) What impact will this leadership change have on your professional career?

The first part of this book addressed many of these questions. Department chairs need to use the trade-off strategies presented in chapter 7 to find a more holistic balance in their lives; chapter 7 illuminates the "dark side" of the department chair position. The intention is not to discourage you from continuing to seek the challenges of academic leadership, but help you recognize, prepare for, and overcome unforeseen trade-offs. This chapter highlights the positive side of the position and discusses: the payoffs that give balance to your professional life, how to gauge the legacy you will leave, and how to develop yourself as an academic leader.

PAYOFFS: REWARDS OF THE POSITION

Chapters 6 and 7 may have illuminated the "dark side" of chairing a department, but most department chairs expressed satisfaction with their jobs. They noted many rewards and benefits that came with serving their colleagues and departments. Serving as department chair must have some significant rewards that counterbalance the frustrations. What are they?

Most would say privately that status and prestige come with the position. But to admit to their faculty colleagues that they enjoy the job causes suspicion. As Dressel points out: "A scholar is not expected to seek or enjoy the position of chair" (1970, 82). If, in fact, one appears to enjoy the assignment or maintain it for several terms, one is suspected of leaving one's discipline for the comfort of administration to justify a lack of scholarly contributions (Moses and Roe 1990). In public, chairs are reluctant to admit the payoffs of administration; it is "unwise, even indecent, because it means one is proclaiming oneself as administrator, whereas most [chairs], especially those on short term appointments, are anxious to remain, and to be seen to be, academics rather than administrators" (Moses and Roe 1990, 209). The position of chair is not perceived by many as a career move, but as a temporary service to the institution and profession.

In private, however, chairs speak candidly about the rewards they receive. From interviews of one hundred department heads in Australia (Moses and Roe 1990) and two national surveys of 1,600 chairs in the United States (Gmelch, Carroll, Seedorf, and Wentz 1990; Gmelch, Burns, Carroll, Harris, and Wentz 1992), and from hundreds of department chair seminars from 1990 to 2010, chairs resoundingly testified about the benefits and payoffs of department leadership. While many of their testimonies overlap, six areas of reward emerge:

Financial reward. Of the chairs in our study, 72 percent received an administrative stipend averaging 12 percent of their salaries, or an average stipend of $3,432. In Australian universities, the financial compensation ranged from as little as $360 per annum up to nearly $7,000. While money alone does not seem to motivate professors to become chairs, it does represent a partial payoff for dealing with the demands of the job. The primary source of satisfaction for chairs actually comes from non-monetary rewards, since the financial stipend is usually modest.

Personal sense of achievement. Chairs who derived a sense of personal achievement from their position expressed it this way: "When I see results of my efforts realized," "when I experience a victory," or "when I have the chance to accomplish something positive."

Personal sense of power. While similar to personal achievement, satisfaction from the ability to have and exercise power emerged as a separate and distinct motive. Although not readily apparent to some chairs and embarrassing to others, many enjoyed the ability to exercise power—especially as it enabled them to direct the department and propagate their own ideas. Their feelings about this satisfaction ranged from the most blatant ("I enjoy power") to the most subtle ("Leading, guiding developments in the department is the reward. I initiated new developments, set it all up, and now I'm enjoying it") (Moses and Roe 1990, 214).

Altruistic satisfaction. Chairs often spoke of their pleasure in "opening doors of opportunities" and "making the job easier" for others, as well as helping them achieve their goals—"made everyone feel good about their own professional development." In a faculty-team sense, they expressed satisfaction with being able to develop a collegial atmosphere where they "increased the level of civility" and "kept the peace without too many serious mistakes."

Departmental success. Chairs also received great satisfaction from building a quality program by "creating a pathway to a stronger department through strategic planning." Some chairs used the seaworthy captain analogy by expressing the satisfaction of maintaining their programs under rough seas: "the ship is still afloat," and "I kept a leaking life boat afloat without throwing anyone to the sharks." Others simply said they "held the fort," "kept the place from falling apart," and "maintained a high quality program in a time of major financial crisis."

Personal growth. Many chairs expressed gratitude for what the chair position had done for them. They learned on the job and received a broader perspective from which to view the college, university, and educational environment, and had the opportunity to test some of their "latent" leadership skills. Approximately 20 percent of chairs used their experience to move into higher levels of administration. While most expressed satisfaction with their personal growth opportunities, it must also be remembered that 65 percent of the chairs did return to faculty status after serving as chair (Carroll and Wolverton 2004).

THE CHAIR LOOP: HOW LONG IS LONG ENOUGH?

Most chairs feel they've plateaued at some point, whether it is after four, six, or more years. Being competent is not enough to keep the fire alive. Remaining a department chair too long results in losing interest in the job, failing to keep up with changes in your discipline, not keeping up with your scholarship, and possibly entering a performance plateau—a chair doom loop (Gmelch 2004; Hollander 1991), as portrayed in Figure 8.1. New chairs enter Quadrant I with a steep learning curve as they learn new skills and find new interests. The "new chairs" progress to the "good chairs" as they become committed to the position and competent in their duties (Quadrant II). The confident chairs now in Quadrant II are careful not to go over the edge and down the slide to becoming a "damn chair" (Quadrant III) or a "doomed chair" (Quadrant IV). Chairs talk about the conditions that influenced the feeling of being plateaued: the *repetition and routine* of tasks where the scenery started looking the same; the diminishing *rate of return* on their investment of time and energy; a decline in their *learning curve*; an *atrophy in their skills*; and feeling, after five or six years' *time* in the office, that they were not making a significant difference.

How do long-serving chairs keep their interest and stay on the edge of advancement? Several types of tactics might help keep the fire alive. *Tinker tactics* can be used to stretch new skills and learn new ideas through new assignments, committees, commissions, team members, and faculty. Many chairs focus on re-treading challenges inside the college and university rather than retreating to another institution. Other chairs practice *toehold tactics* by searching outside the department, college, or institution for new challenges from professional associations, national organizations, and interdisciplinary connections. Zigzag chairs explore *mosaic tactics* to look for greener grass in other professions, such as national and state agencies or full-time consulting. Finally, some chairs use *exploration tactics*: they realize that, for them, being a department chair is not enough, and seek a deanship. Chairs can search inside, outside, across, and beyond their current position and institution to prevent plateauing and keep their fires alive.

Most long-serving department chairs feel plateaued at some point; these seven survival skills can help keep chairs alive in their jobs: 1) communicate in all directions—to the dean and central administration, faculty, staff, students, and external stakeholders; 2) realize that being a chair is not about you, but about serving others; 3) know yourself by seeking feedback and expressing your values and beliefs to others; 4) enhance leadership and learning through seminars, conferences, reading, and exploration; 5) relate well to others, especially your dean; 6) hallucinate, get a vision; and 7) love being a chair or leave it, life is too short to do it just for the perks, assuming there are any!

Former chairs advise those still in the trenches to keep the vision alive, advance the college, hire well, keep good faculty, continue to lead, give back to the profession, and have fun! Many chairs had words of advice for those new to the position (Gmelch and Mitchell 2008). Possibly motivated by their need for generativity or just generosity, here is what they shared:

1. Be clear why you want to be a chair.

2. Become centered in your philosophy, values, and beliefs.

Figure 8.1 The Leader Loop: "Zoom to Doom"

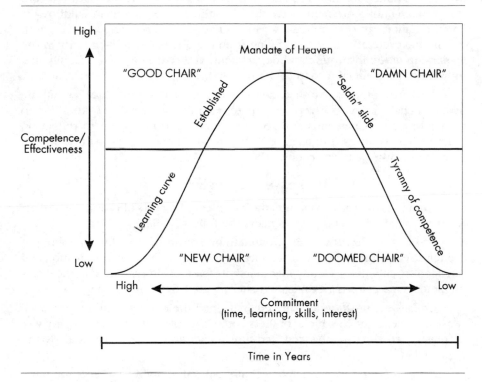

3. Pay attention to national issues in your profession.
4. Develop a university-wide perspective.
5. Build a multilayered support network.
6. Develop your team.
7. Identify a mentor.
8. Take time for professional development.
9. Establish a strong academic record.
10. Play well with others—collaborate.
11. Find personal/professional and scholar/leader balance.
12. Take care of yourself—physically, socially, and intellectually.

DID YOU MAKE A DIFFERENCE?

Typically, chairs serve six years, after which they follow one of two paths. Approximately one of every five chairs moves upward in academic administration and completes the full transition from faculty to administration. Most chairs do not continue in administration, returning instead to faculty status, where they remain until retirement. "Like the springtime observations of wildflowers and dormant creatures, there is a sense of a natural, undirected process at work ....The life cycle of chairs is emerging from faculty, being active briefly in the leadership of the institution and department, and returning to the faculty in a more dormant leadership state" (Carroll 1990, 117).

This metaphor may be an accurate portrayal of department leadership. Inevitably, chairs leave. Is it your destiny to return to scholarship or to go on to higher levels of management? Before you leave, you may want to reflect on whether you've made a difference. What do you hope others in your department will think you have accomplished?

Leave your legacy

Hundreds of chairs from our studies reflected on this question and collectively viewed their accomplishments in the following light.

Productive climate. Chairs wanted to be known for developing a sense of academic excitement, providing faculty with opportunities for gratification and satisfaction, enhancing faculty members' professional lives, reducing the stress on faculty, and restoring peace and fostering growth among faculty.

Collegial atmosphere. Many chairs hoped their faculty felt an improved sense of collegiality, in which conflicts could be healed, the level of civility was increased, morale was enhanced, and some peace and order was brought to the department.

Program advancement. Many chairs aspired to build a national program, bring the department into the twenty-first century, focus the department's area of concentration, enhance the department's reputation, increase the department's status within the university, upgrade the department's teaching and research, build better relations with the field, and modernize the curriculum and physical facilities.

Quality staffing. Many chairs wanted to leave a legacy of recruiting and developing competent faculty, especially by promoting women and minorities and nurturing young faculty members.

Quality leadership. Chairs reflected on their personal qualities and hoped they would be respected for their honesty, openness, fairness, justice, and altruism. They also sought to provide the vision and strategic direction needed to advance the mission of the department into the next century. As a summary note, one chair hoped the faculty would say that "he accomplished most of what he said needed to be done, and did it with integrity."

If you had to write your legacy today, what would it be?

DEPARTMENT CHAIR DEVELOPMENT

Chairs experienced socialization processes similar to those undergone by other academic leaders (individual, informal, random, and variable), not the professionals they are often empowered to prepare. Socialization of academic leaders appears to be left to chance. Institutions must realize the impact socialization techniques can have on productivity, as well as a chair's inclination toward longevity with or departure from the institution.

Because many department chairs' initial training is in academic research and teaching, they rarely anticipate the roles and responsibilities of chairing a department, and have had minimal management and leadership training. One of the most glaring shortcomings in the leadership area is the scarcity of sound research on the training and development of leaders (Conger and Benjamin 1999).

Train for leadership

It is well known that few chairs receive training to prepare and maintain leadership skills. The value of leadership is too great not to invest in it. Both managerial skills and leadership perspectives are needed to meet the challenges facing higher education. Table 8.1 lists the areas, as identified by chairs, in which training is most needed.

In order to keep from losing your balance when you assume leadership, consider some of these ideas for re-imagining the role of department chair. While the future of academic leadership may be plagued by the paradoxes inherent in the position, it is also replete with rewards and challenges. This book was written to assist you in understanding your role as department leader and developing the skills necessary to enjoy your faculty, reap the rewards, and lead your department into the twenty-first century.

The leadership development of chairs is a process that extends over many years, spanning all the seasons of professional life. As discussed in chapter 1, our research suggests three spheres essential to developing chairs: 1) a *conceptual understanding* of the unique roles and responsibilities encompassed by academic leadership; 2) the *skills* necessary to achieve results through working with faculty, staff, students, other administrators, and external constituents; and 3) the practice of *reflection* to learn from past experiences and perfect the art of leadership.

In the final part of this book, we will highlight and detail strategies that can foster department chair leadership development in each of these three spheres at three levels of interventions—institutional, professional, and personal (a 3x3 matrix in Table 8.2). At the *institutional level*, we define the scope of the job through systemic efforts and seamless approaches to the selection, socialization, and development of department chairs. Prior to and while serving as chair, universities must provide for continued professional leadership development

---

Table 8.1 Areas in which Chairs Indicate Most Need for Training

---

1. Evaluating faculty performance
2. Maintaining conducive work climate (reducing conflicts among faculty)
3. Obtaining and managing external funds (grants, contracts)
4. Preparing and proposing budgets
5. Developing and initiating long-range departmental goals
6. Managing department resources (finances, facilities, equipment)
7. Encouraging professional development activities of faculty
8. Managing non-academic staff
9. Planning and evaluating curriculum development
10. Providing informal faculty leadership
11. Ensuring the maintenance of accurate departmental records
12. Recruiting and selecting faculty

---

through such strategies such as in-house retreats, personalized professional development plans, and periodic reviews and renewals (sabbaticals). At the *professional level*, organizations such as the Council for Colleges of Arts and Sciences (CCAS), the American Council on Education (ACE), and the American Association of Colleges of Teacher Education (AACTE) must provide forums, conferences, and literature to guide chairs in dealing with strategic issues in the academy and deanship. Finally, at the *personal level*, chairs need assessment, feedback, personal advice, and other means to become effective leaders. On a personal basis, chairs need to engage in networking, seeking mentors, coaching opportunities, and practicing reflective writing.

In the last section of this chapter we highlight strategies to foster department chair leadership- development. Table 8.2 provides a visual display of these strategies. We have grouped them under the three components of leadership development—conceptual understanding, skill development, and reflective practice—and across three levels of interventions—personal, institutional, and professional. The policy implications and recommendations come from interviews with department chairs and from the leadership intuition of the authors as practicing scholar-leaders.

1. Development of conceptual understanding: Habits of mind

Cognitively, chairs must explore and understand leadership by using mental models, frameworks, and role theory to reveal leadership's many dimensions. In other words, they must form new *habits of the mind* as they move from specialists to generalists. They must understand how universities operate, i.e., the unique organizational, political, and social characteristics of institutions of higher education. Two issues surfaced during the interviews with the chairs:

Table 8.2 Strategies for Chair Leadership Development

Leadership Development Component			
Levels of Internention	Conceptual Understanding *Habits of Mind*	Skill Development *Habits of Practice*	Reflective Practice *Habits of Heart*
Personal	• Higher education classes • Leadership conferences • Books and journals • Shift in mental models	• External seminars (ACE) • Assessment of skills and fit • Support groups • Short commercial seminars • Executive MBA/MPA	• Journaling • Reflective practice • Mentors/coaches/networks • Values clarification • faith
Institutional	• Orientation process • Seamless socialization • Leadership development • Administrative sabbatical • Team indoctrination • Professional stipend	• Campus leadership seminars • Internships & shadowing • Mentorships • Campus chairs • Colleague-chairs off campus • Professional development	• Annual reviews • Chairs' council • Chair-dean 1/1 sessions • Campus confidants • Chairs' therapy sessions • Mentor programs
Professional	• Generic HE organizations • New chairs' institute • Chair associations • networks	• Leadership literature • Chair-a-like organizations • Conference workshops • Professional organizations	• Internet networks • Consortia • Regional, state, national networks • National cohort programs

1) as chairs moved into leadership positions, the concept of the job shifted; 2) although some commonalities were seen to exist across all types of organizations, chairs in institutions of higher education faced challenges not typical of managers and leaders in other organizations. As academics move into leadership positions, they start to perceive themselves differently. For example, using Bolman and Deal's terms (1991), and the work of researchers from Iowa State University, department chairs predominantly think in terms of their human and structural frames of leadership. As the chairs we studied moved into department leadership, two new frames, the political and symbolic, emerged and demanded greater attention (Gmelch, Reason, Schuh, and Shelly 2002).

Personal Level. Department chairs can expand their conceptual understanding of the position by attending classes on higher education leadership,
honing their skills in such areas as budgeting, strategic planning, curriculum development, and current issues. The *Chronicle of Higher Education* and other
higher education trade magazines, as well as academic journals, also provide
chairs with critical background and perspectives on higher education issues. In
addition, chairs can attend general higher education conferences such as the
American Council on Education (ACE), American Association of Colleges for
Teacher Education (AACTE), and American Association of Colleges and Universities (AAC&U). These and other associations also feature workshops, presentations, and symposia on higher education administration. Several chairs reported
that these conferences provided them with an environmental scan of higher education as they moved from a disciplinary specialist to a university generalist.
These and other efforts can aid chairs in gaining a better grasp on how others go
about balancing management with leadership, scholarship with leadership, and
personal life with professional life.

Institutional Level. Universities and colleges need to design and deliver
programs to address the seamless selection, socialization, and development of
chairs. Some institutions with unique missions, such as land-grant universities
and faith-based institutions, have developed systematic team meetings designed
to understand and advance their unique market position and core beliefs. For
example, Iowa State University instituted a systematic leadership development
program on campus that brought in higher education scholars to provide them
with an understanding of how universities work. Another (faith-based) institution had monthly readings and discussion with the president, vice president,
and deans on what it meant to be a Jesuit university.

Few chairs reported having a formal orientation to the university as a new
chair. An orientation session would have provided a more seamless socialization into the institution. Such a process would incorporate training across all
phases of chair acclimation. Universities need to systematically invest in and formally train their future leaders. They need to think about "growing" their own
chairs, cultivating promising academic leaders and spotting them early on in
their academic careers, as many corporations have done. These organizations
have "built to last" over the years by developing their own executives from
within (Collins and Porras 1994). During the chairship, universities must provide for continued professional leadership development through in-house retreats; allocate professional development stipends to allow chairs to take
advantage of workshops, seminars, books, and journals; and assist with professional leaves after a designated number of years of service as an academic administrator.

Professional Level. Chairs rely on general higher education organizations
such as AAC&U, CCAS, AACTE, and ACE in developing their conceptual understanding of higher education and how universities work. In addition, disci-

pline-specific seminars, such as the three day AACTE or ACE Chairs' Institute, help orient newly appointed chairs. Other professional organizations also provide specific conferences and institutes to socialize chairs and facilitate networking among them. Many chairs who were more senior in their tenure or had moved out of their roles spoke of training future generations of chairs by mentoring, counseling, and teaching.

2. Skill development: Habits of practice

It is not uncommon to hear someone say, "That person is a natural leader." The observation is usually made about an individual who seems to know, intuitively, the right approach to every situation. In reality, born leaders are few. Most, including those who have accepted being a chair, need instruction, experience, nurturing, and time to develop the skills they need. They develop through *habits of practice*.

The dilemma for chairs as leaders arises because the necessary components of skill development are seldom, or insufficiently, available. Chairs quickly realize that the expertise and behaviors they need to be successful leaders will be acquired—for the most part—piecemeal, while they are on the job. It seems ironic that the individuals upon whom our colleges and universities rely most for leadership are essentially self-taught. Their skills develop gradually and often haphazardly, the result of arbitrary training, inadequate feedback, and random mentoring.

Personal Level. A personal development plan starts with an assessment of the match between the types of skills chairs bring to the position, the demands of the job, and the job's fit with the institution. Chairs unfamiliar with managerial subtleties need to seek out opportunities to hone their executive skills, but the majority develop their leadership skills on their own, with little or no formal training or assistance. Many rely on management literature, poring over books and articles that offer administrative models and management strategies. Even then, the tasks that veteran chairs have learned to manage can stymie inexperienced leaders. Lacking knowledge and skills, many rely on trial-and-error problem-solving, an approach that can frustrate faculty who want decisive leaders with ready solutions.

The professional development market is replete with commercial venues for management seminars, from performance evaluation to principled negotiations. These individual programs tend to be relatively short, from half-day seminars to ones lasting a few days, with little or no follow-up. Not so abundant are skill development programs tailor-made for academic leaders. A chair with the time and the money—e.g., a professional development stipend—can find many opportunities for executive development.

Institutional Level. Institutions can encourage professional development through the office of Human Resources. A few institutions provide in-house workshops and seminars that focus on real-life leadership and campus issues.

However, few tailor their programs to executive development. Most programs are designed for middle management and address managerial issues, personnel practices, legal issues, and budget development, not the difficult leadership and ethical dilemmas often plaguing chairs. One institution has a year-long professional development program designed to stimulate and sustain skill development through practice and reinforcement of key executive skills. Other institutions have provided executive internships and exchanges across colleges and campuses for up-and-coming university administrators. Sitting chairs typically can't take advantage of these opportunities, as they are constantly in the line of fire.

In-house mentorships are another avenue of skill development for chairs. A new chair should have a mentor—someone who can listen and help with decisions. Unfortunately, it's typical for the more experienced chairs or deans who could mentor novice leaders to be unavailable, or seen as a risk. Developing chairs may shy away from asking their more experienced colleagues for help. They worry that their lack of knowledge will be perceived as weakness. However, pairing seasoned and new chairs in a safe environment has provided some chairs with a "critical friend" in whom to confide. Internships, shadowing experiences, and exchanges developed by universities to facilitate skill acquisition also provide a venue for dean development.

Professional Level. Skill development opportunities are minimal; of those that do exist, few provide systematic preparation or follow-up. If funding and time allows, some deans attend workshops or institutes offered by professional education organizations; others undergo specific managerial training like that offered by Harvard or Bryn Mawr; still others attend conferences focused on some particular aspect of administration, like those presented by CASE. Within colleges and schools, chairs from similar institutions have formed separate organizations to further their discussions and address common problems. Organizations such as the Council for Colleges of Arts and Sciences (CCAS) and the American Assembly of Collegiate Schools of Business (AACSB) also provide conferences and institutes to socialize their chairs into their leadership positions.

Overall, chairs who maintain active membership in broad-based professional organizations reap the benefit of learning more generalized approaches to academic leadership than they did from their specialized, discipline-centered professional organizations (Wolverton and Gmelch 2002). Many chairs don't believe there is much to read about leading a department, but leadership has become a discipline in its own right, within which chairs must hone their skills. From professional associations' annual meetings, publications, and networks, chairs can learn the language, literature, and innovations of higher education (Green and McDade 1994).

3. Development through reflective practice: Habits of heart

Understanding the roles and possessing the requisite skills are not enough for chairs to believe they can be successful. Leadership development is for many an inner journey, often the most difficult part of professional growth. Self-knowledge, personal awareness, and corrective feedback are all part of a leader's development. Moral, ethical, and spiritual dimensions, or *habits of the heart*, tend to have a major impact on a department chair's ability to complete the leadership journey. Leadership development is very much about finding one's voice (Kouzes and Posner 1987). In the words of many chairs, because credibility and authenticity lie at the heart of leadership, determining and identifying guiding beliefs and assumptions lie at the heart of becoming a good chair. Therefore, providing structured feedback, promoting reflection, and developing self-awareness are critical strategies that enable chairs to flourish.

As reflected in Table 8.1, institutions, professions, and chairs themselves must build in time and mechanisms to become reflective practitioners.

Personal Level. While managers reflect in action, seldom do they reflect on their reflection-in-action (Schon 1983). Hence, their reflection, a crucially important dimension of chair development, tends to remain inaccessible to others. Chairs end up feeling alone: they have no lines of communication with colleagues whose jobs are similar. No one understands them. Moreover, because awareness of one's intuitive thinking usually grows out of practice in articulating it to others, chairs' relative isolation cuts off their access to their own reflection-in-action.

Some reflective activities in which chairs can engage are those that involve imprinting their professional experience, such as journaling or personal dictation. Chairs believe reflection helps them weigh their careers against their personal lives. Faith and value-clarification also provide some chairs with an inner sense of commitment and fulfillment. These core values help them face new challenges every day and give them a fresh spirit.

Institutional Level. Leadership development does not take place in a vacuum. It flourishes best within a group, or with trusted colleagues acting as mentors, partners, and coaches. Institutions employ such formal structures as the chairs' council, academic partnerships, and annual reviews to provide chairs with systematic means of formative evaluation and feedback. Many chairs also develop an informal chairs' group that meets without the dean over coffee or a meal in a "safe" environment, so they may reflect and explore common issues. For many, these become therapy sessions. One-on-one conversations with the dean also provide space for discussing a variety of topics, from campus issues to the meaning of life. For some, having a confidant outside the college creates a supportive bonding experience that guides the exploration of ethical and moral dilemmas.

Professional Level. Professional organizations help chairs establish networks. Through attending national conferences and professional development programs, chairs get connected with their colleagues, form personal relationships, and develop networks of confidants. Like the freshman experience in college, freshman chairs attending the Chairs' Institute form bonds with other new chairs that last throughout their tenure and beyond. They meet annually and keep in touch via phone and email throughout the year. By helping chairs across institutions, states, and countries consider what it is they really do, how they do it, why they do it, and what difference they make, professional organizations go a long way toward creating and supporting a cadre of effective campus leaders.

CONCLUSION

To become an expert takes time. Research suggests it takes 10,000 hours of practice to become an expert (Gladwell 2008). Studies of executives in the corporate world who attain international levels of performance point to the ten-year rule of preparation (Ericsson, Drampe, and Tesch-Romer 1993). In the academy, we believe it takes a professor seven years to become proficient and tenured, and up to fourteen years to become a full professor of international stature. Chairs should be no different, but they only serve six years on the average. Lines of succession for chairs are unclear, and chairs' relatively high turnover rate (one in five, annually) suggests that we do not groom our leaders in ways that promote longevity, success, and effectiveness. For this reason alone, higher education can ill afford the luxury of almost total inattention when it comes to preparing department chairs—for today, as never before, universities and colleges need competent leaders.

REFERENCES

Aldag, R. J., and B. Joseph. 2000. *Leadership and vision*. NY: Lebhar-Friedman Books.

Alfred, R., et.al. 2006. *Managing the big picture in colleges and universities: from tactics to strategy*. Westport, CT: ACE/Praeger.

Alinsky, Saul D. 1971. *Rules for radicals: A practical primer for realistic radicals*. New York, NY: Random House.

Amit, R. C., C. Lucier, M. A. Hitt, and R. D. Nixon. 2002. Strategies for creating value in the entrepreneurial millennium. In *Creating value: Winners in the new business environment*, edited by M. A. Hitt, R. C. Amit, C. Lucier, and R. D. Nixon. Oxford, UK: Blackwell.

Andrews, Kenneth R. 1987. *The concept of corporate strategy*, 3rd ed. Homewood, IL: Richard D. Irwin.

Badaracco, Joseph L. 1997. *Defining moments: When managers must choose between right and right*. Boston, MA: Harvard Business School Press.

———. 2003. *Negotiation*. Boston, MA: Harvard Business School Press.

Bare, Alan C. 1980. The study of academic department performance. *Research in Higher Education* 12 (1).

——— 1986. Managerial behavior of college chairpersons and administrators. *Research in Higher Education* 24 (2):128-138.

Barney, J. B., and A. M. Arikan. 2001.The resource based view: origins and implications. In *Handbook of Strategic Management*, edited by M. A. Hitt, R. E. Freeman, and J. R. Harriosn. Oxford, UK: Blackwell Publishers.

Bass, Bernard M. 1985. *Leadership and performance beyond expectations*. New York, NY: Free Press.

Beineke, John A., and Roger H. Sublett. 1999. *Leadership lessons and competencies: Learning from the Kellogg National Fellowship Program*. Battle Creek, MI: Kellogg Foundation.

Bennis, Warren G., and Burt Nanus. 1985 *Leaders: The strategy for taking charge*. New York, NY: Harper and Row.

Bennis, Warren G., Kenneth D. Benne, and Robert Chin. 1969. *The planning of change,* 2nd ed. New York, NY: Holt, Rhinehart, and Winston.

Bligh, M. C., and J. R. Mendl,. 2005. The cultural ecology of leadership: an analysis of popular books. In *The Psycology of Leadership: New Perspectives on Leadership*, edited by D. M. Messick and R. M. Kramer. Mahwah, NJ: Erlbaum.

Bolman, Lee G., and Terrence E. Deal. 2003. *Reframing organizations,* 3rd ed. San Francisco, CA: Jossey-Bass.

Bowman, R. F., Jr. 2002. The real work of department chair. *The Clearing House,* 75 (3):158-162.

Boyatzis, Richard E. 1990. Beyond competence: The choice to be a leader. Paper presented at the Academy of Management Meetings, at San Francisco, CA.

Bridges, W., and S. Mitchell. 2000. Leading transition: A new model for change. *Leader to Leader.* 16 (1):30-36.

Buller, Jeffrey L. 2006. *The essential department chair: A practical guide to college administration.* Bolton, MA: Anker Publications.

Burke, J. C. 2005. *Achieving accountability in higher education: Balancing public, academic, and market demands.* San Francisco, CA: Jossey-Bass.

Caplan, Robert D., S. Cobb, J. R. P. French, R. Van Harrison, and S. R. Pinneau. 1980. *Job demands and worker health: Main effects and occupational differences.* HEW Publication No. N10SH: 75-160.

Carroll, James B. 1990. Career paths of department chairs in doctorate-granting institutions. Ph.D. diss., Washington State University.

Carroll, James B., and Mimi Wolverton. 2004. Who becomes a chair? In *The life cycle of a department chair,* edited by Walter H. Gmelch and John H. Schuh. San Francisco, CA: Jossey-Bass.

Chu, Don. 2006. *The department chair primer: Leading and managing academic departments.* Bolton, MA: Anker Publishing.

Cleveland, Harlan. 1985. *The knowledge executive: Leadership in an information society.* New York, NY: Dutton.

Coleman, M. S. 2004. Implementing a strategic plan using indicators and targets. In *Pursuing excellence in higher education: Eight fundamental challenges,* edited by B. D. Ruben. San Francisco, CA: Jossey-Bass.

Collins, James C., and Jerry I. Porras. 1994. *Built to last: Successful habits of visionary companies.* New York, NY: Harper Business.

Conger, Jay A. 1992. *Learning to lead: The art of transforming managers into leaders.* San Francisco, CA: Jossey-Bass.

Conger, Jay A., and Beth Benjamin. 1999. *Building leaders: How successful companies develop the next generation.* San Francisco, CA: Jossey-Bass Publishers.

Corwin, Ronald G. 1969. Patterns of organizational conflict. *Administrative Science Quarterly.* December: 507-520.

Creswell, John W., et al. 1990. *The academic chairperson's handbook.* Lincoln, NE: University of Nebraska Press.

Diamond, R. M., ed. 2002. *Field guide to academic leadership.* San Francisco, CA: Jossey-Bass.

Diebold, John. 1984. *Making the future work.* New York, NY: Simon and Schuster.

Dooris, M. J. 2002/2003. Two decades of strategic planning. *Planning Higher Education,* 31 (2):26-32.

Dressel, Paul L., Frank C. Johnson, and Phillip M. Marcus. 1970. *The confidence crisis.* San Francisco, CA: Jossey-Bass.

Drucker, Peter F. 1974. *Management: Tasks, responsibilities, practice.* New York, NY: Harper and Row.

Dyer, William G. 1977. *Team building: Issues and alternatives.* Reading, MA: Addison-Wesley.

Eckel, Peter, Madeleine Green, and Barbara Hill. 2001. *Riding the waves of change: Insights from transforming institutions*. Washington D.C.: American Council on Education.

Ericsson, K. Anders, Ralf T. Krampe, and Clemens Tesch-Romer. 1993. The role of deliberate practices in the acquisition of expert performance. *Psychological Review*, 100 (3):363-406.

Ericsson, K. Anders, and Jacqui Smith. 1991. *Towards a general theory of expertise*. Cambridge: Cambridge University Press.

Eunson, Baden. 1997. *Dealing with conflict*. Brisbane, Australia: John Wiley and Sons.

Fisher, Roger, and Daniel Shapiro. 2005. *Beyond reason: Using emotions as you negotiate*. London, England: Penguin Books.

Fisher, Roger, and William L. Ury. 1983. *Getting to yes: Negotiating agreement without giving in*. New York, NY: Penguin Books.

Foskett, N., and J. Lumby. 2003. *Leading and managing education*. Thousand Oaks, CA: Sage.

French, John R. P., Jr., and Bertram Raven. 1968. The bases of social power. In *Group dynamics: Research and theory*, edited by Dorwin Cartwright and Alvin F. Zander. New York, NY: Harper and Row.

Friedman, Meyer, and Ray H. Rosenman. 1974. *Type A behavior and your heart*. New York, NY: Alfred A. Knopf.

Gardner, John W. 1987. *Leadership development*. Washington, DC: Independent Sector.

Gladwell, Malcolm. 2008. *Outliers: The story of success*. New York, NY: Little, Brown, and Company.

Gmelch, Walter H. 1982. *Beyond stress to effective management*. New York, NY: John Wiley and Sons.

Gmelch, Walter H. 1991. *Paying the price for academic leadership: Department chair tradeoffs*. *Educational Record* 72 (3):45-49.

———. 1991. Sources of stress for academic department chairs: A national study. Paper presented at the American Educational Research Association Conference, Chicago, IL. (ERIC:ED 339 306).

———. 1993. *Coping with faculty stress*. Newbury Park, CA: Sage Publications.

———. 1995. Department chairs under siege: Resolving the web of conflict. In *Conflict Management in Higher Education*, edited by Susan A. Holton. San Francisco, CA: Jossey-Bass.

———. 1998. The Janus syndrome: Managing conflict from the middle. In *Mending the Cracks in the Ivory Tower*, edited by S.A. Holton. Bolton, MA: Anker Publications.

———. 2000a. Building leadership capacity for institutional reform. *Academic Leadership Connection* 7 (1):1-6.

———. 2000b. Leadership succession: How new deans take charge and learn the job. *Journal of Leadership Studies*, 7 (8):68-87.

———. 2002. *Deans balancing acts: Education leaders and the challenges they face*. Washington, DC: AACTE Publications.

———. 2003. *Seasons of a dean's life: Passages of the profession — keeping the fire alive*. American Association of Colleges for Teacher Education, New Orleans, LA.

———. 2004. The department chair's balancing acts. In *The life cycle of a department chair*, edited by Walter H. Gmelch and John H. Schuh. San Francisco, CA: Jossey Bass. No 126.

Gmelch, Walter H., and John S. Burns. 1993. The cost of academic leadership: Department chair stress. *Innovative Higher Education* 17 (4):259-270.

————. 1994. Sources of stress for academic department chairs. *Journal of Educational Administration* 32 (1):79-94.

Gmelch, Walter H., John S. Burns, James B. Carroll, S. Harris, and D. Wentz. 1992. *Center for the study of the department chair: 1992 survey*. Pullman, WA: Washington State University.

Gmelch, Walter H., and James B. Carroll. 1991. The three R's of conflict management for department chairs and faculty. *Innovative Higher Education* 16 (2):107-121.

Gmelch Walter H., James B. Carroll, R. Seedorf, and D. Wentz. 1990. *Center for the study of the department chair: 1990 survey*. Pullman, WA: Washington State University.

Gmelch, Walter H., and B. Houchen. 1994. The balancing act of community college chairs. *Academic Leadership* 2:4-11.

Gmelch, Walter H., Nicholas P. Lovrich, and Phyllis K. Wilke. 1984. Stress in academe: A national perspective. *Research in Higher Education* 20 (4):477-490.

————. 1984. A national study of stress among university faculty members. *Phi Delta Kappan*, 64 (5):367.

Gmelch, Walter H., and Val D. Miskin. 1984. *Productivity teams*. New York, NY: John Wiley and Sons.

————. 1993. *Leadership skills for department chairs*. Bolton, MA: Anker Press.

————. 1995. *Chairing an academic department* . Newbury Park, CA: Sage Publications.

————. 2004. *Chairing an academic department*, 2nd ed. Madison, WI: Atwood Publishing.

Gmelch, Walter H., and Forrest W. Parkay. 1999. Becoming a department chair: Negotiating the transition from scholar to administrator. Paper presented at American Educational Research Association Conference, Montreal, Canada, April.

Gmelch, Walter H., Robert D. Reason, John H. Schuh, and Mack C. Shelley. 2002. *The call for academic leaders: The academic leadership forum*. Iowa State University, Iowa: Center for Academic Leadership.

Gmelch, Walter H., and James C. Sarros. 1996. How to work with your dean: Voices of American and Australian department chairs. *The Department Chair: A Newsletter for Academic Administrators*. 6 (4), 1:19-20.

Gmelch, Walter H., and John H. Schuh, eds. 2004. *The life cycle of a department chair*. San Fransisco, CA: Jossey Bass.

Gmelch, Walter H., and R. Seedorf. 1989. Academic leadership under siege: The ambiguity and imbalance of department chairs. *Journal for Higher Education Management*, 5:37-44.

Gmelch, Walter H., and Phyllis K. Wilke. 1991. The stresses of faculty and administrators in higher education. *Journal for Higher Education Management*, 6 (2):23-31.

Green, Madeleine F., and Sharon A. McDade. 1994. *Investing in higher education: A handbook of leadership development*. Phoenix, AZ: Oryx Press.

Greiff, Barry S., and Preston K. Munther. 1980. *Tradeoffs: Executive, family, and organizational life*. New York, NY: New American Library.

Gunsalus, C. K. 2006. *The college administrator's survival guide*. Cambridge, MA: Harvard University Press.

Hall, Jay, and Martha S. Williams. 1966. A comparison of decision-making performances in established and ad hoc groups. *Journal of Personality and Social Psychology*, February: 214-222.

Hax, Arnoldo C., and Nicholas S. Majluf. 1991. *The strategy concept and process: A pragmatic approach*. Englewood Cliffs, NJ: Prentice-Hall.

Hecht, Irene W. D. 2004. The professional development of department chairs. In *The life cycle of a department chair*, edited by Walter H. Gmelch and John H. Schuh. San Francisco, CA: Jossey-Bass.

Hecht, Irene W. D., Mary Lou Higgerson, Walter H. Gmelch, and Alan Tucker. 1999. *The department chair as academic leader*. Phoenix, AZ: Oryx Press.

Higgerson, Mary Lou. 1996. *Communication skills for department chairs*. Bolton, MA: Anker Publications.

Higgerson, Mary Lou, and Teddi A. Joyce. 2007. *Effective leadership communication*. Bolton, MA: Anker Publications.

Hollander, Dory. 1991. *The doom loop system*. New York, NY: Viking Penguin.

House, R. J., and M. L. Baetz. 1979. Some empirical generalizations and new research directions. In *Research in organizational behavior*, 1: 341-423B, edited by M. Staw. Greenwich, CT: JAI Press.

Huffman, J. 2002. The role of shared values and vision in creating professional learning communities. *NASSP Bulletin*, 87 (637):21-34.

Kahn, Robert L., Donald M. Wolfe, Robert P. Quinn, J. Diedrick Snoek, and Robert A. Rosenthal. 1964. *Organizational stress: Studies in role conflict and ambiguity*. New York, NY: John Wiley and Sons.

Katzell, Raymond A., and Richard A. Guzzo. 1983. Psychology approaches to productivity improvement. *American Psychologist*, 38: 468-472.

Katzenbach, Jon R. 1998. Teams at the top. Boston, MA: Harvard Business School Press.

Katzenbach, Jon R., and D.K. Smith. 1993. *The wisdom of teams*. Boston, MA: Harper Business.

Keys, Bernard, and Thomas Case. 1990. How to become an influential manager. *Academy of Management Executive,* 3: 38-51.

Kouzes, James M., and Barry Z. Posner. 1987. *The leadership challenge: How to get extraordinary things done in organizations*. San Francisco, CA: Jossey-Bass.

Larson, Carl E., and Frank M. J. La Fasto. 1989. *Team work: What must go right/what can go wrong*. Newbury Park, CA: Sage Publications.

Latham, Gary P., and Timothy P. Steele. 1983. The motivational effects of participation versus goal-setting on performance. *Academy of Management Journal* 18: 824-845.

Latham, Gary P. and Gary A. Yukl. 1975. A review of research on the application of goal-setting in organizations. *Academy of Management Journal* 18: 824-845.

Lawler, Edward E., III. 1986. *High-involvement management: Participative strategies for improving organizational performance*. San Francisco, CA: Jossey-Bass.

Lazarus, Richard S. 1966. *Psychological stress and the coping process*. New York: McGraw-Hill.

Leaming, D. 2003. *Managing people: A guide for department chairs and deans*. Bolton, MA: Anker.

Lee, D. E. 1985. Department chairpersons' perceptions of the role in three institutions. *Perception and Motor Skills*, 61: 23-49.

Lee, N. Douglas. 2006. *Chairing academic departments: Traditional and emerging expectations*. Bolton, MA: Anker Publications.

Lieberson, Stanely, and James F. O'Connor. 1972. Leadership and organizational performance: A study of large corporations. *American Sociological Review,*. 37: 117-130.

Lincoln, W., and R. O'Donnell. 1986. *The course for mediators and impartial hearing officers*. Tacoma WA: National Center Associates.

Lucas, Ann F. 1994. *Strengthening departmental leadership*. San Francisco, CA: Jossey-Bass.

Mackenzie, A. 1990. *The time trap*. New York, NY: AMACOM.

McLaughlin, G. W. M., L. R. Malpass, J. R. Montgomery, and L. F. Malpass. 1975. Selected characteristics, roles, goals, and satisfactions of department chairmen in state and land-grant institutions. *Research in Higher Education*, 3: 243-59.

Meredith, G. M., and M. A. Wunsch. 1991. The leadership of department chairpersons: Time resource management, rewards, frustrations, and role satisfaction. *Psychological Reports*, 68: 451-454.

Milstein, M. 1987. *Dilemmas in the chairpersons' role and what can be done about them*. Pullman, WA: Center for the Study of the Department Chair, Washington State University.

Miskin, Val D., and Walter H. Gmelch. 1985. Quality leadership for quality teams. *Training and Development Journal*, 39 (5):122-30.

Moore, C. W. 1996. *The mediation process: Practical strategies for resolving conflict*. San Francisco, CA: Jossey-Bass.

Morrill, R. L. 2007. *Strategic leadership: Integrating strategy and leadership in colleges and universities*. Westport CT: Praeger Publishers.

Moses, I., and E. Roe. 1990. *Heads and chairs: Managing academic departments*. Queensland, Australia: University of Queensland Press.

Nanus, B. 1992. *Visionary leadership*. San Francisco, CA: Jossey-Bass.

Oncken, W., Jr., and D. L. Wass. 1974. Management time: Who's got the monkey? *Harvard Business Review*. 52 (6):75-80.

Parker, G. M. 1991. *Team players and teamwork*. San Francisco, CA: Jossey-Bass.

Priem, R. L., and J. E. Butler. 2000. Is the source-based view a useful perspective for strategic research? *Academy of Management Review*, 26: 22-40.

Raiffa, Howard. 1982. *The art and science of negotiation*. Cambridge, MA: The Belknap Press of Harvard University Press.

Robbins, S. P. 1974. *Managing organizational conflict*. Englewood Cliffs, NJ: Prentice-Hall.

Rosser, V. J., L. K. Johnsrud, and R. H. Heck. 2003. Academic deans and directors: assessing their effectiveness from individual and institutional perspectives. *Journal of Higher Education*, 74 (1):1-25.

Rost, J. 1995. Leaders and followers are the people in this relationship. In *The Leader's Companion*, edited by J. T. Wren. NY: Free Press.

Schön, Donald A. 1983. *The reflective practitioner: How professionals think in action*. New York, NY: Basic Books.

Seedorf, R. 1990. *Transition to leadership: The university department chair*. Ph.D. diss. Pullman, WA: Washington State University.

Senge, P. M. 1990. *The fifth discipline: The art and practice of the learning organization*. New York, NY: Doubleday/Currency.

Sessa, V. I., and J. J. Taylor. 2000. *Executive selection: Strategies for success*. San Francisco, CA: Jossey-Bass.

Selye, H. 1974. *Stress without distress*. Philadelphia, PA: J.G. Lippincott company

Shaw, K. A. 2006. *The international leader*. NY: Syracuse University Press.

Shulman, L. 2007. Counting and recounting: Assessment and the quest for accountability. *Change*, January/February: 20-25.

Simmel, G. 1955. *Conflict*. New York, NY: Free Press.

Smart, J., and J. Elton. 1976. Duties performed by department chairmen in Holland's model environments. *Journal of Educational Psychology*, 68 (2):194-204.

Smith, J. E., K. P. Carson, and R. A. Alexander. 1984. Leadership: It can make a difference. *Academy of Management Journal*. 27: 765-776.

Steiner, G. A. 1979. *Strategic planning: What every manager should know.* New York: Free Press.

Thomas, K. W. 1976. Conflict and conflict management. In *Handbook of industrial and organizational psychology*, edited by M. D. Dunnette. Chicago, IL: Rand McNally.

Thomas, K. W., and R. L. Kilmann. 1974. *Thomas-Kilmann conflict mode instrument*. Xicom Inc.

Thomas, J. R., and John H. Schuh. 2004. Socializing new chairs. In *The life cycle of a department chair*, edited by Walter H. Gmelch and John H. Schuh. San Francisco, CA: Jossey Bass. No 126.

Thomas, M. D., and W. L. Bainbridge. 2002. Sharing the glory. *Leadership*, 31 (3):12-15.

Thompson, A. A., A. J. Strickland III, and J. E. Gamble. 2005. *Crafting and executing strategy*. New York, NY: McGraw-Hill/Irwin.

Trainer, J. F. 2004. Models and tools for strategic planning. In *Successful Strategic Planning: New Directions for Institutional Research*, edited by M. J. Dooris, J. M. Kelley, and J. F. Trainer. San Francisco: Jossey-Bass.

Tucker, A. 1992. *Chairing the academic department: Leadership among peers*. 3rd ed. Phoenix, AZ: American Council on Education/Oryx.

Tuckman, B. W. 1955. Development sequence in small groups. *Psychological Bulletin*, 63 (6): 384-99.

Ury, William. 2007. *The power of a positive no: How to say no and still get to yes*. New York, NY: Bantam Books.

Vroom, V. H., and A. G. Jago. 1988. *The new leadership*. Englewood Cliffs, NJ: Prentice-Hall.

Westley, F. 1992. Vision worlds: Strategic visions as social interaction. *Advances in Strategic Management*, 8: 271-305.

Walton, R. E., and J. M. Dutton. 1969. The management of interpersonal conflict: A model and review. *Administrative Science Quarterly*, March: 73-84.

Wergin, Jon F. 2003. *Departments that work: Creating and sustaining cultures of excellence in academic departments*. Bolton, MA: Anker Publishing.

Weiner, N., and Thomas A. Mahoney. 1981. A model of corporate performance as a function of environmental, organizational, and leadership influences. *Academy of Management Journal*, 24: 453-470.

Westley, F. 1992. Vision worlds: Strategic visions as social interaction. *Advances in Strategic Management*, 8: 271-305.

Wheeler, Daniel W., et al. 2008. *The academic chair's handbook*. 2nd ed. San Francisco, CA: Jossey-Bass.

Wilke, Phyllis K., Walter H. Gmelch, and Nicholas P. Lovrich, Jr. 1985. Stress and productivity: Evidence of the inverted U-function. *Public Productivity Review*, 9 (4):342-356.

Williams, M. J., Jr. 1985. The management of conflict. In *Applying corporate management strategies: New dimensions for higher education*, edited by R. J. Fecher. San Francisco, CA: Jossey-Bass.

Wolverton, Mimi, and Walter H. Gmelch. 2002. *College deans: Leading from within*. Westwood, CT: Oryx Press.

Yavitz, B., and W. H. Newman. 1982. *Strategy in action*. New York, NY: Free Press.

Yukl, G. A. 1981. *Leadership in organizations*. Englewood Cliffs, NJ: Prentice-Hall.

INDEX

INDEX

M

management molecule 80-81, 81, 84
management team. *See* management molecule
measurable goals 57, *58*, *59*, *85*
mediation 27-28, 81, 89, 92, 111-113
mission. *See* vision
mission statement. *See* vision/mission statement

P

performance
  plateau 152, 153
  strategies 152-153
principled conflict resolution 94, 105-109, *108*, *109*, *110*
  definition 106
professional development 141-144, 146-147, 150
  academic 141-144, 146-147, 150
  administrative 156-162
  as stressor 146, 178
professional organizations 158-159, 160

R

reflective practice 20-22, 156, 160-162
  definition 20
  reflection-in-action 20-22, 161

S

Schön, Donald 21
skill development 19-20, 156, *157*, 159-160
  definition 19
spheres of development 18-22, *20*, 155, *157*
  conceptual understanding 19, 156-159
  reflective practice 20-22, 160-162
  skill development 19-20, 159-160
staff
  action planning 73-74
  conflict 97
  goal setting 64-66, 65
stakeholders 39-41. *See also* constituencies
stress 77, 120
  balancing 141-144
  Chair Stress Cycle 119-120, *120*
  Chair Stress Inventory *121-122*, 122, *127-128*

common myths concerning 118-119
common stressors *121-122*, 122-124, *129*
conflict as source of 90, *92*
consequences of 126, 138, *139*
coping with Type A behavior 131-132
identifying stressors 121-126, *125*, *127-128*
perception of 126
time as source of 78, 80, 133
Type A characteristics 128-131, *130*, *132*
stress management
  action planning 138-141, *140*, *142*

  strategies 134-138, 139-141, *140*, *142*
SWOT analysis 41-43, *44*. *See also* department analysis

T

team culture 23, 28, 29-36
  assessing 30, *30*
  building 29, 30, 31-36, *32*
  definition 29-30, *32*
  goals 25, *33*
team development
  barriers to 28-29
  stages of 26-28, *27*
team leadership 23-24, 26-28, 31, 33-34, 36-37
Thomas, Kenneth W. 99, 100, 101
time as stressor 78, 80, 133, 141, 143
time management 77-78
  balance in 141-144
  control in 79-80
  delegation and 80, 81-82
  faculty/staff interactions 86-87
  formal meetings 78, 84-87, *85*, *87*
  HIPO activities 145-146
  LOPO activities 146
  personal decisions and 87
  unplanned interruptions 78, 80-82, *83*
transition from faculty to administration 11-15, *15*, 77-78, 141, 154, 157-158
Tucker, Allan 9, 26
Tuckman Model 26-28, 27
Type A behavior 126-131, *131*
  coping with 131-133
  worksheet *132*

U

Ury, William L 105, 106

173

About the Authors

WALTER H. GMELCH is currently Dean of the School of Education at the University of San Francisco. Just prior to this appointment, he was Dean of the College of Education at Iowa State University and before that, served in the roles of Interim Dean, Associate Dean, Department Chair and Professor at Washington State University. Gmelch also directed the National Center for Academic Leadership. He earned a Ph.D. in the Educational Executive Program from the University of California (Santa Barbara), a masters in Business Administration from the University of California (Berkeley), and a bachelors degree from Stanford University.

As educator, management consultant, university administrator, and former business executive, Gmelch has conducted research and written extensively on the topics of leadership, team development, conflict, and stress and time management. He has published over 100 articles, 20 books, and 200 scholarly papers in national and international journals. Gmelch has authored books on department leadership with Val Miskin and others (*Chairing an Academic Department, The Life Cycle of a Department Chair, and Productivity Teams: Beyond Quality Circles*), college leadership (*The Changing Nature of the Academic Dean, Deans' Balancing Acts, College Deans: Leading from Within, and The Seasons of a Dean's Life*), and stress management (*Coping with Faculty Stress and Beyond Stress to Effective Management*).

Today Gmelch is one of the leading researchers in the study of academic leaders in higher education, serving as editor of two journals and as well as the editorial board of several other journals including *The Department Chair, Innovative Higher Education, Academic Leadership,* and the *Center for Academic Leadership Newsletter*. During the 1990s he directed two national studies of 1,600 university department chairs in the United States, one study of 1,580 Australian department heads, another investigation of 1,000 community college chairs, and also has completed an international study of 2,000 academic deans in Australia and America.

Gmelch has received numerous honors including a Kellogg National Fellowship, the University Council for Educational Administration Distinguished Professor Award, the Faculty Excellence Award for Research, and the Education Press Award of America. In addition, he served on the Danforth Leadership Program and as an Australian Research Fellow.

VAL D. MISKIN is Director of Graduate Programs in the College of Business at Washington State University. He received his Ph.D. in administration from Washington State University, an M.B.A. from Utah State University, and a bachelor's degree in psychology from Brigham Young University. A one time business owner, he has more than 15 years of corporate managerial experience in management training and leadership development. He has presented papers at the national meetings of the Academy of Management, the National Conference of Entrepreneurial Studies, and the National Chairpersons Conference. His work has appeared in the *American Society for Training and Development Journal, Personnel, Frontiers of Entrepreneurship Research, The Journal of Staff, Program, and Organization Development,* and The *Journal of Small Business Strategy.* He is coauthor of *Productivity Teams: Beyond Quality Circles, Productivity and Team Building: How Groups Become Teams,* and *Charing an Academic Department.* He currently teaches in the areas of strategic leadership and human resource management. He has conducted hundreds of leadership seminars and strategic management workshops over the years, and he regularly provides consulting services to both business and nonprofit organizations.